Views on the News

Views on the News

The Media and Public Opinion

Edited by
Michael P. Beaubien and John S. Wyeth, Jr.

The Chet Huntley Memorial Lectures

NEW YORK UNIVERSITY PRESS
New York and London

Copyright © 1994 by New York University
All rights reserved
Manufactured in the United States of America

Publication of this book was made possible by NBC News; Mr. Harold Levine; the firm of Levine, Huntley, Schmidt, and Beaver, Inc.; and New York University.

The sponsors of the Chet Huntley Memorial Lecture series wish to thank Elisa A. Guarino, Video Producer and Press Officer, Office of Public Affairs, New York University, for organizing and managing the lecture series.

Photo credits: p. viii, James Salzano; p. x, courtesy of Harold Levine; pp. xii, 42, 44, 72, 76, 10, 172, 192, 206, courtesy of NBC News; pp. xiv, xvi, xvii, 4, courtesy of Tippy Huntley Conrad; pp. 1, 14, 22, 23, 39, 50, 52, 55, 64, 69, 86, 95, 97, 99, 109, 111, 115, 123, 133, 147, 165, 169, 181, 184, 187, 196, 203, 204, 216, courtesy of AP/Wide World Photos; pp. 6, 102, 126, 150, courtesy of New York University Photo Bureau; p. 8, courtesy of CBS News; p. 44, courtesy of Anthony Lewis; p. 130, courtesy of Henry Grunwald; p. 154, courtesy of ABC Photography Department; p. 174, courtesy of Tom Wicker; p. 190, courtesy of Esquire; p. 208, courtesy of Rupert Murdoch

Library of Congress Cataloging-in-Publication Data

Views on the news: the media and public opinion / edited by Michael P. Beaubien and John S. Wyeth, Jr.
    p.   cm.
    Collection of lectures presented at the Chet Huntley Memorial lectures at New York University, 1979–1990.
    ISBN 0-8147-3510-X
    1. Television broadcasting of news—United States. 2. Huntley, Chet, 1911–1974—Biography. I. Beaubien, Michael P. II. Wyeth, John S. III. Chet Huntley Memorial lectures.
PN4888.T4G65   1994
070.1′95—dc20   93-43679
                                                                                            CIP

New York University Press books are printed on acid-free paper, and their binding materials are chosen for their strength and durability.

Contents

Introduction by L. Jay Oliva — ix

Foreword by Harold Levine — xi

Preface by Lester Crystal — xiii

Chet Huntley: A Biography by Margaret Rooney — xv

1 **Agnew Plus Ten**
   Perspective — 1
   Introduction of Richard Salant by
      Tippy Huntley Conrad — 4
   Presentation by Richard Salant — 9

2 **The Press and the Presidency**
   Perspective — 39
   Introduction of Anthony Lewis by John Chancellor — 42
   Presentation by Anthony Lewis — 45

3 **The Nightly News: A Leap of Faith versus the Bottom Line**
   Perspective — 69
   Introduction of Fred W. Friendly by Lester Crystal — 72
   Presentation by Fred W. Friendly — 77

4 **Private Wars: The Government and Press Censorship**
   Perspective — 97
   Introduction of John Chancellor by Elizabeth Drew — 102
   Presentation by John Chancellor — 105

5 **Absence of Malice: Libel as Press Censorship**
   Perspective — 123
   Introduction of Henry Grunwald by
      Larry Grossman — 126
   Presentation by Henry Grunwald — 131

Contents

6 **The Image versus the Word: Good and Bad Television News**
    Perspective — 147
    Introduction of Diane Sawyer by Larry Grossman — 150
    Presentation by Diane Sawyer — 155

7 **Choosing a President: Are Media Part of the Problem?**
    Perspective — 169
    Introduction of Tom Wicker by Tom Brokaw — 172
    Presentation by Tom Wicker — 175

8 **Freedom and Responsibility: The Burden of the First Amendment**
    Perspective — 187
    Introduction of Tom Brokaw by Edward Kosner — 190
    Presentation by Tom Brokaw — 193

9 **Crime, the Masses, and Media Responsibility**
    Perspective — 203
    Introduction of Rupert Murdoch by Michael Gartner — 206
    Presentation by Rupert Murdoch — 209

Our liberty depends on the freedom of the press,
and that cannot be limited without being lost.
                                    Thomas Jefferson

Introduction

I am very pleased, on behalf of our entire university community, to express our appreciation for the privilege of hosting, from 1979 until 1990, the Chet Huntley Memorial Lectures at New York University.

Located in a city that is one of the world's principal centers of journalism, the university maintains numerous links to the communications industry, including the leadership of trustees who serve as chief executive officers for national television networks; the professional contributions of thousands of alumni; and the expertise of many colleagues of the academic community who are also working journalists.

The university holds a treasured, lifelong tradition of providing to the public a forum for strong opinion, vigorous debate, and the free exchange of ideas. The Chet Huntley Memorial Lectures have been a valuable part of that commitment. It is also fitting that the series has been housed in a university that offers its students such a strong program in newspaper, magazine, and broadcast journalism.

We are greatly indebted to the initiative and vision of Harold Levine, who first proposed a series of lectures in memory of his friend and colleague; to Lester Crystal, then president of NBC News, who provided strong personal and institutional support; and, of course, to Tippy Huntley Conrad for her encouragement and wise counsel in helping to develop the series.

We take pride in being able to offer to the larger community this body of work by journalists of extraordinary achievement, who presented wide-ranging, keenly insightful analyses of some of the most important issues of our time. The quality of their lectures is true to the highest standards of excellence that mark the legacy left us by Chet Huntley.

Our guests tackled exceedingly tough questions and provided some useful answers. We are delighted that their thoughts were first shared with our community of learners and that they now form this collection, published by the New York University Press. It is both a privilege and a pleasure to recommend it to you.

L. Jay Oliva
Washington Square
June 1993

Foreword

Chet Huntley and I met in 1970 at the home of a friend. Chet had already left NBC, and was involved in developing the resort in Big Sky, Montana. At the time, I owned a small New York advertising agency, and Chet asked me to help market and advertise Big Sky. He expressed a real interest in my plans to acquire the agency I was working for, and in March 1972 we announced the fomation of Levine, Huntley, Schmidt Advertising.

From that time until his untimely death, Chet attended client meetings, visited with prospects, and addressed industry conferences. I attribute much of the success of our agency to Chet's principles. If Chet Huntley had not become a journalist, he could have been a successful advertising man. He wrote superbly, and had a unique understanding of the consumer. I recall his telling our staff in the very beginning, "If you show respect for the consumer the consumer will respect your message and your client's product."

Because of his special contribution to the world of broadcast journalism and his unique contribution to our agency, I met with Lester Crystal, then president of NBC News, to discuss the idea of a lecture series in Chet's memory. He indicated that NBC would participate and agreed that it should be held at New York University so that students of journalism would be able to learn from the series.

We contacted Dr. John Sawhill, then president of New York University, and arranged for the agency, now named Levine, Huntley, Schmidt, and Beaver Inc., to host the lecture series. The first selection committee included myself, Tippy Huntley Conrad, Dr. Sawhill, Mr. Crystal, Seymour Topping of the *New York Times,* and John Chancellor of NBC. It was agreed that each year an outstanding journalist would be invited to speak on whatever topic relating to the press they wished to discuss. The lecture would be open to all university students in addition to guests from print and broadcast media.

I am pleased that succeeding presidents of NBC News and the university continued the series, and that NYU Press is making this book possible. I hope the lectures will inspire young people to maintain a commitment to an open and free press that is so important to the preservation of our democratic society. These are the principles Chet Huntley devoted his life to as a newspaper man and as a broadcast journalist.

Harold Levine
Westport, CT
March 1993

Preface

Chet Huntley's lasting contribution to broadcast journalism is legend. Every history written about the medium will include the prominent role he played in making television news the major information source for a majority of Americans.

When Chet retired we felt an emptiness because we would no longer see and hear him regularly. When he died, that emptiness was magnified. His imprint was everywhere, but those of us close to him asked ourselves: how could his contributions be perpetuated and extended?

I was associated with the "Huntley-Brinkley Report" and its successor program, the "NBC Nightly News," for ten years. I worked directly with Chet from 1967–70 when I was a producer for the program in New York. His professionalism and support profoundly affected my career. So, I was gratified and very enthusiastic when Harold Levine came to me in 1978 and asked me, as NBC News president, to support a Chet Huntley Memorial Lecture Series.

The lecture series was a perfect way to commemorate Chet Huntley's significance to our profession and to extend his contribution by providing a platform for the serious discussion and presentation of issues Chet felt strongly about. The academic context guaranteed its seriousness, its permanence, and its high standard of quality.

Chet Huntley was a pillar of our information age. The lecture series secured that position and gave it a continued life that remains important to us all.

Lester Crystal
Executive Producer, "MacNeil-Lehrer NewsHour"
June 1993

Chet Huntley
(1911–1974)

For almost fifteen years, Chet Huntley's authoritative voice and serious demeanor conveyed the news of the world each night to millions of Americans. Huntley and his less solemn coanchor, David Brinkley, apparently struck a perfect balance in tone and perspective, making "The Huntley–Brinkley Report" television's most popular news program, with an audience estimated at twenty-million viewers. One consumer research study found, in 1965, that this team of journalists was recognized by more adult Americans than were Cary Grant, James Stewart, the Beatles, and John Wayne. And for more than one generation of Americans, Huntley and Brinkley's blend of earnestness and irony and their crisp, on-camera exchange of news items and *good-nights* will always be the irreproachable prototype of television news broadcasting.

"The Huntley–Brinkley Report" was, for Chester Robert Huntley, one phase of a broadcasting career that spanned forty years. That career began at KPCB, a small radio station in Seattle, where he worked during his senior year at the University of Washington. After graduation, and several jobs at other local stations, Mr. Huntley was hired by the NBC affiliate in Los Angeles in 1937. The West Coast remained his base for almost twenty years, and he worked at various times for NBC, CBS, and ABC in Los Angeles.

He joined NBC News in New York in 1955. It was one year later that he and David Brinkley first collaborated—as anchormen for NBC's coverage of the Democratic and Republican National Conventions. A few months later, NBC made this successful collaboration a daily event: "The Huntley–Brinkley Report" replaced John Cameron Swayze on the NBC evening news.

Success did not soften Chet Huntley's convictions on issues of his time—or his inclination to express views that were not universally embraced. In the early 1950s, he was outspoken in his criticism of Senator Joseph McCarthy's reckless charges of Communist allegiance by government officials and private citizens. And in 1967, he crossed a picket line of the American Federation of Television and Radio Artists, contending that "newsmen just don't belong in there with actors, singers, and dancers."

Born in Cardwell, Montana on December 10, 1911, he was the son of a railroad telegrapher. He grew up on his grandfather's sheep ranch in

Chet Huntley

Chet Huntley with his wife Tippy and broadcasting partner David Brinkley.

northern Montana and in a succession of towns throughout the state. He fondly recalled the landscape of his youth, the unspoken lessons about hard work and stamina, and one particularly inspiring high-school teacher in his memoir, *The Generous Years: Remembrances of a Frontier Boyhood*. When he began working at NBC in New York, he installed in his modern office at Rockefeller Center a tangible reminder of his past: the old rolltop desk his father had used when he worked for the Northern Pacific Railroad. Chet Huntley remained active after retirement from his long career in broadcast journalism, pursuing business ventures that climaxed with the creation of The Big Sky Montana project.

Mr. Huntley earned national awards for his reporting on discrimination against Mexican–Americans and on the wartime relocation of Japanese–Americans. Among his numerous honors were two Overseas Press Club Awards, an Alfred I. duPont Award, and a George Polk Memorial Award.

Chet Huntley with General William Westmoreland in Vietnam.

Together with David Brinkley he won eight Emmy Awards and two Peabody Awards. He received a University of Missouri Honor Medal and an honorary Doctor of Letters degree from Franklin and Marshal College. In 1970, he was named "Broadcaster of the Year" by the International Radio and Television Society.

He retired from "The Huntley–Brinkley Report" and from broadcasting in July 1970, leaving his television audience with this entreaty and this hope: "Be patient and have courage—there will be better and happier news some day, if we work at it."

Chet Huntley died March 20, 1974 at Big Sky, Montana.

Margaret Rooney

1

Agnew Plus Ten

November 15, 1979

Perspective

Before Lyndon Johnson left the presidency in 1969, he gave the incoming vice president, Spiro Agnew, a few words of advice on dealing with the press. "Young man," Johnson reportedly said, "we have in this country two big television networks, NBC and CBS. We have two news magazines, *Newsweek* and *Time*. We have two wire services, AP and UPI. We have two pollsters, Gallup and Harris. We have two big newspapers, the *Washington Post* and the *New York Times*. They're all so damned big they think they own the country. But, young man, don't get any ideas about fighting." Despite these words of advice, Agnew became one of the country's most outspoken critics of the press during his term as vice president. Richard S. Salant's lecture, the first in the Chet Huntley Memorial Lecture Series, chronicles the "grand conspiracy" by the Nixon-Agnew administration to undermine freedom of the press. More than any other prior presidential administration, he asserts, Nixon and Agnew sought to level direct attacks against the press—particularly against the broadcast press—since the government's regulatory powers are stronger over television and radio than over the print media.

The First Amendment of the United States Constitution has traditionally been the protector of the press, stating as it does that "Congress shall make no law . . . abridging freedom of speech, or of the press." The press was perceived as a watchdog over public officials, charged not only with informing the public, but with ensuring that abuses of power do not go unrecognized. This view of the press as a "Fourth Estate," as an essential part of the country's social and political system, was held by the founders of the United States to be fundamental to the well-being of the republic. In 1791 the only medium of the press was print, which was operated entirely as a private enterprise despite its influence in the public sector. With the advent of broadcast media in the twentieth century, however, a double standard emerged. The print media remained unregulated, but the government required the licensing of all radio and television stations. The airwaves, according to the government, belonged to the public, and were thus open to regulation.

In addition, the government has been permitted to take programming content into account in the decision to license radio and television broadcasters. Beginning with the Radio Act of 1927, Congress regulated the time and frequency of broadcasts, as well as their political content. Regulation by the Federal Communications Commission (FCC) required stations to allot equal time to opposing viewpoints, particularly on controversial issues. Salant notes as examples the 1969 case of *Red Lion Broadcasting Co.* v. *FCC,* and the complementary case, *Miami Herald Publishing Co.* v. *Tornillo.*

The *Red Lion* case arose after a radio station refused to allow the author of a book critical of Arizona Senator Barry Goldwater to respond to an attack on his work. The U.S. Supreme Court upheld the author's right to equal time, substantially diminishing the ability of broadcasters to program material that might be seen as controversial. Print media, on the other hand, had no such restrictions. In the *Miami Herald* case, the U.S. Supreme Court argued that the decision to give equal time was a matter of "editorial control and judgment," at least within the realm of the print media.

In most cases, Salant concedes, high-level government officials tolerate freedom of the press, although they may have "very unkind things to say" about the press from time to time. But he points out instances in which the Nixon administration—in particular Vice President Agnew—verbally threatened the press and, perhaps even more frightening, used FCC regulations to "bring to heel" the press for its own political survival.

The Nixon-Agnew administration, in the midst of widespread anti-Vietnam sentiment, blamed the press for creating and spreading negative opinions of the President. Agnew spoke on the subject at a Midwest Republican Conference in Des Moines, Iowa, in November 1969, challenging newspeople to come "down from their ivory towers to enjoy the rough and tumble of public debate." His populist rhetoric suggested that newspeople were elitist Eastern liberals who were unwilling to engage with the masses in genuine public debate.

Working with the FCC, the Nixon administration tried to censor the press. Although, as Salant points out, the government could often attack print media as well as broadcast media, since a number of large conglomerates owned both types, television was considered to be the most dangerous medium by Nixon, Agnew, and their associates, who used intimidation tactics to keep broadcasters in line. Richard Salant's lecture, "Agnew Plus Ten," chronicles the Nixon-Agnew war on the press with chilling clarity, demonstrating how easily such tactics could have led to a devastating erosion of First Amendment rights—and how they still could.

Introduction of Richard S. Salant by Tippy Huntley Conrad

Tippy Huntley Conrad, the widow of broadcast journalist Chet Huntley, has been a driving force behind this memorial lecture series dedicated to her husband. Formerly Lewis Tipton Stringer, she was a nightly weathergirl at Washington, D.C.'s WRC-TV when she met Huntley in the late 1950s. Also an actress and singer, she was married to actor William Conrad, who died recently. She introduced former CBS News executive Richard S. Salant.

Introduction

*H*istorically, whether inscribed in the walls of caves or printed on pulp for world distribution, it has been the birthright of the press to keep society informed. With the advent of television, many people have been wooed from the effort of reading to the ease of watching the news. That reality, coupled with the cost-efficient television advertising dollar, has destroyed a substantial segment of the independent press as we have known it. Competition from television has forced some dailies to combine into chains, often merging, in self-defense, with radio and television stations. Other newspapers, in order to survive, have become information banks, supplementing their sales with telex displays, computer printouts, or microfilm reproductions. Satellites, lasers, facsimiles—they're all modern miracle by-products of newsprint.

But technology can either inundate us with minutiae, or select the significant. Editing out the trivial, the sensational, and the irrelevant in the search for truth is the ultimate responsiblity for newspeople in all the media. Television, in particular, has an even greater responsibility, because, for so many, television news is all the news there is.

Chet knew his duty—to keep the public informed. He resented the time given to sensationalism, and the treatment of news as entertainment. He was sensitive to the size of the television audience, and its wide range of intelligence. To Chet, the art of news writing was to design a simple, declarative sentence, and the craftsmanship of news commentary was to deliver that sentence with sincerity and conviction. For him, the blend of these skills was essential for holding public attention and earning the public trust.

Cet took a sabbatical from television news broadcasting. He wanted to find a better way to report and comment in depth

Agnew Plus Ten

Richard S. Salant and Tippy Huntley Conrad at the Chet Huntley lecture.

on the matters which truly affected the lives of his audience. This lecture series is designed to find that better way.

This evening, we have with us an experienced and innovative leader in the television industry—a person with exemplary communications credentials, who spent the last quarter of a century trying to improve the quality of commercial news broadcasting. The fine print on Richard Salant's contract, as a new vice president, or rather—it's a longer title than that—as a new senior executive of NBC, is still wet.

After 25 productive years in television, he has earned the title of vice chairman of the Board of Directors of the National Broadcasting Company. But Dick Salant's roots are in television news broadcasting. In 1952, he left a career in the law to join CBS, and in 1961, he headed up CBS News and developed landmark programming, such as the "CBS Evening News" with Walter Cronkite, the CBS News Election Unit, the "CBS Morning News," "60 Minutes," and so many more. The quality of Dick Salant's performance is best measured by his peers. This year alone, he received the Gold Medal Award from the International Radio and Television Society, the George Polk Award from the Society of Professional Journalists, and the George Foster Peabody Award for leadership and the staunch defense of a free press. It follows that Dick Salant was unanimously chosen by our committee to inaugurate the Chet Huntley Memorial Series.

Richard S. Salant

Born April 14, 1914, in New York City, Richard S. Salant earned bachelor and law degrees at Harvard University before passing the bar in New York in 1938. After a 14-year career as attorney both for the U.S. government (1938–43) and in private practice, he accepted (1952) a postion as vice president of CBS. Despite the fact that he had never been a journalist by profession, Salant served as president of CBS News from 1961–64 and from 1966–79. During his tenure, the nightly news report saw an expansion from 15 to 30 minutes, a shift that heralded a new respect for broadcast journalism. He introduced "CBS Morning News" and "Sunday Mornings," and made a point of separating the news department from sports and entertainment programming. In 1968 he created the multiple Emmy award-winning "60 Minutes," which has stood at the top of network ratings since its inception. A winner of numerous awards for excellence in broadcast journalism, Salant left CBS in 1979 to become the vice chairman of the Board of Directors for NBC. He died of heart failure on February 16, 1993.

Agnew Plus Ten

I am immeasurably grateful for the opportunity to deliver the inaugural Chet Huntley Memorial Lecture. In permitting me to participate in honoring Chet, you flatter me. I am grateful. Chet is a man indeed to be honored.

But the fact is—Chet, I hardly knew him. I admired him, I respected him, and since our world of network broadcast journalism is, above all, competitive, I didn't like him a bit. With David Brinkley—and behind the camera, Reuven Frank—Chet gave me sleepless nights and my CBS bosses fits. I hated to be second, and so he gave me a pain in my pride. He was too good.

The man who, professionally, knew Chet best—my brilliant colleague, Reuven Frank—said it best, as Reuven so often does. It would be foolish for me to try to say it differently. The best I can do is simply to recall to you some of what Reuven said about Chet on March 26, 1974, in NBC studio 6-A.

> I remember how rarely he got angry, how easy it was to tell when he was angry. He did not hide his angers or cherish them. He did not know how to be devious. He was bad at getting rid of pests, at refusing favors, at saying no. Bill McAndrew once said to me, if Chet was a woman, he would always be pregnant. He was always doing something for somebody.
>
> He was without envy—at the peak of his fame he was unpretentious. He never told me the inside story of anything. He was the easiest man I ever worked with, he liked to work, and his physical capacities were prodigious. He would fly all night, and work 12 or 15 hours the next day, and help carry the gear and be gracious to everybody, and still be going when the rest of us

had given out. He knew everybody he worked with, and never kept himself apart from them.

We who worked with him, especially in those early days, came from all over, but we were mostly city boys. He taught us about the West, his attitudes, his absolute openness, his optimism.

Chet was born December 10, 1911, in Cardwell, Montana. He lived in Saco, Scoby, Willow Creek, Logan, Big Timber, Norris, Whitehall, Bozeman, Reedpoint—all in Montana. He went to Montana State College and then to the University of Washington. He worked as a waiter, a window washer, a telegram delivery boy. His first job in broadcasting was in 1934 at KCBC in Seattle. He was paid $10 a month, his laundry service was free, and he traded sponsorship accounts for food. He wrote, and broadcast, the news.

He went to CBS on the West coast in 1938—at $65 a week. In 1951, he shifted to ABC—and criticized Senator Joseph McCarthy, for which somebody denounced Chet as a Communist. Chet sued—and won $10,000. He never collected the money. He said he "didn't want it, but the judgment still stands to keep the party from opening her mouth again."

In 1955, Chet came to NBC. In 1956, he and David Brinkley coanchored the Democratic and Republican Conventions. On October 29, 1956, the "Huntley-Brinkley Report" was first broadcast. "Good night, David." "Good night, Chet." Good night for too long a while from where I was sitting—good night CBS News.

What I knew about Chet from watching and listening to him at a distance has been confirmed these last few weeks from talking to his associates about him, and from reading about him. He was an open man who listened—superb characteristics that make a great journalist. Just as important, he was an independent man. As Fred Ferretti wrote in the *New York Times* on the eve of Chet's retirement, "A paternal descendant of John Adams and John Quincy Adams, Huntley reeks of independence." When Chet was toying with the idea of running for political office, he said, "I'm a registered independent. I don't subscribe to the ideology of either party."

He didn't just say he was independent. In his professional life, he lived it. In the crucial formative days of broadcast journalism, when the broadcast newsroom could have become home for a gaggle of entertainers, or even worse, a plaything, an instrument of a broadcast station owner's own political biases or business objectives, it was Chet who recognized early on that unless any such catastrophe was stopped in its tracks, there would never be any such craft, or profession, as broadcast journalism at all. Thus it was that in the late forties, it was Chet, as founder and member of the Radio News Club, who spearheaded the battle against a powerful radio station owner who commanded, on pain of dismissal, that his news employees slant the news to fit the owner's political, economic, and social biases. And on October 18, 1950, Chet was a witness before the FCC in the case against the owner, and he provided the key testimony.

It was a landmark case. It was, for those times, an act of courage. It was an act of independence. It was a critical step in setting that infant, broadcast journalism, on the fork in the road marked professionalism and integrity.

Typical of his independence and courage, in the face of the scorn of many of his colleagues, insisting on going his own way whatever the peer group pressures, was his decision in 1967, when the American Federation of Television and Radio Artists, the union of which broadcast newsmen were members, struck and picketed the networks. Most news personnel stayed away from work during the strike. Not Chet. He went through picket lines at Rockefeller Center, from which he broadcast, and he stayed at work. "Newsmen," Chet said at the time, "just don't belong in there with actors, singers, dancers and announcers, and I wasn't about to stand still and be pushed around. . . . I was damned if they were going to push me into anything."

Whether his associates and his peers agreed with him is irrelevant. Whether he was right or wrong is irrelevant. He saw what he saw, thought what he thought, and did what he thought he had to do, proving once again, as Ed Murrow had proved, that great journalists cannot be made—first, they have to be born as great journalists. And that means having the kind of fierce independence and integrity that Chet had.

No nattering Nabob or effete Easterner, was Chet.

And so it was inevitable that Chet should have been bluntly outraged by Vice President Spiro Agnew's rhetoric. "Spiro Agnew," Chet said, "is appealing to the most base of elements. All the networks broke their asses putting his famous Des Moines speech on television. We almost created him, for god's sake. . . . I resent being lumped in with his eastern establishment effete intellectuals. I've had more cow manure on my boots than he ever thought of."

And that brings us to Agnew—what he did, whom and what it all represented, and what, in the perspective of ten years, it seems to have meant. Only in a narrow sense is it all done with, and gone. It was, I suggest, more—far, far more—than a brief and temporary aberration of a single individual—Agnew—in this nation's political life, off on an ugly frolic of his own. For that reason, and because it all came to us piece by sometimes unrelated piece, it is useful to review it—not to pick at old scabs, but to see what it tells us about the government, the people, and the press—especially broadcast journalism.

Agnew—and those who, as we shall see, so clearly put him up to it—*can* happen again. We who cherish a free press were lucky then. If it does, heaven forbid, happen again, will we be so lucky again? We didn't escape Agnewism on the merits. We escaped almost by chance—through an extraordinary seres of accidents, from the discovery by a building custodian of a taped door, to the happenstance that two young *Washington Post* reporters named Woodward and Bernstein on the local beat had nothing else to do and so were hanging around the *Post* newsroom that night in June when the Watergate break-in happened, to the assignment of the ensuing case to a tough and stubborn judge named Sirica, to the nearly accidental discovery of the White House tapes. In fact, were it not for the excesses of the Nixon administration, including the tapes, we might never have known. And Nixon would have remained President until 1976—his plans against the press brought to fruition instead of being aborted.

Agnew Plus Ten

Spiro Agnew began his attack on the press with a speech in Des Moines, Iowa, on November 13, 1969.

It isn't often that people make their own smoking pistols. Next time they may not.

And so, let's go back, and see what happened and what we can learn—back to exactly ten years and two days ago, when the first cannonballs were shot across our bow. The place—Des Moines, a regional Republican meeting; the date—November 13, 1969; the context—Vietnam, and an enormous erosion of popular support for the war. Lyndon B. Johnson, fatally hurt by what had come to be called a credibility gap and by the domestic divisions arising out of the Vietnam War, had decided not to run for reelection. And, it is reasonable now to speculate, Nixon and his associates, after Nixon was elected President, wanted to make sure that no such thing would happen to them. They were determined to end the dissent. And so the press, which they regarded as the cause, not the mirror, of the dissent, had to be brought to heel.

On November 3, 1969, ten days before Agnew's Des Moines speech, President Nixon had addressed the nation on all four television networks, reviewing the war, his efforts to bring it to an end, and rejecting U.S. withdrawal, fixing the blame for the war's continuance on the North Vietnamese. Each of the networks followed the address with summary, analysis, and discussion. The Nixon administration was displeased—very displeased—with these post-address broadcasts.

I remember well the mid-afternoon of November 13, 1969. I was at a meeting when an advance script of Agnew's speech, scheduled for seven o'clock that evening, was brought in. We read it quickly. We immediately decided to make arrangements to broadcast it live. So did the other networks. The test has to be—and it was—newsworthiness. That was an easy news judgment, even if it may have seemed to have been an exercise in masochism.

Agnew, in his Des Moines speech, charged that critical comments—he called them "instant analysis and querulous criticism"—following a presidential address might unduly influence the American people. The views of network television newspersons, he said, did not represent the views of America. Only a handful of men, located in the east and inbred, who "talk constantly to one another" decide what is news, and what the people will and will not see and hear. Television, he said pointedly, is "enjoying a monopoly sanctioned and licensed ('licensed'—mark that word) by government." He suggested that were it not for television, there would be no marches or demonstrations. "It is time," he warned, "that the networks were made (again—mark that word 'made') more responsive to the views of the nation." He didn't specify just who would do the making. But it took no imagination to know who. For he reminded us all of what we needed no reminding—the Supreme Court's decision, a few months before, in the *Red Lion* case, holding that broadcast journalism had considerably lesser rights than the print press—and that a broadcaster's license—his right to stay in business—including journalism—could be withheld or revoked for what the broadcaster does, or does not do, in the field of news and information. By the *Red Lion* case, the law of the land became, simply, that the government could regulate broadcast news in ways, and to an extent, that are unthinkable, under the First Amendment, if sought to be applied to print. Indeed, we learned some years later from the Supreme Court's decision in the *Tornillo* case, that a statutory right of reply, upheld in *Red Lion,* could not be constitutionally applied to a newspaper.

In any event, on November 20, 1969, in Montgomery, Alabama, Agnew came back to the attack—and broadened it to include print as well as broadcasters. His print targets were the *Washington Post* and the *New York Times*—both critical of the Nixon administration. And he returned to his attack on network news. He said that when "the network commentators go beyond fair criticism, they will be called on to defend their statements . . . and when their criticism becomes excessive or unjust, we shall invite them down from their ivory towers to enjoy the rough and tumble of public debate."

Again, Agnew didn't specify. He didn't spell out who would do the "calling" of the commentators to defend themselves, or before whom they would be called. He didn't identify the "we" who would do the inviting to "the rough and tumble of public debate"—or with whom they were to debate. He didn't explain by whose standards the fairness of the newsmen's comments and the justness of their criticism were to be judged, or who would be the judges. It wasn't hard to guess—the federal government, Nixon's administration.

That Agnew protested, in his November 13 speech, and repeated three times on November 20, that he was not advocating censorship, gave us no comfort. On the contrary, as Dr. Frank Stanton said, five days after the Montgomery speech,

> It is far more shocking to me that the utterances of the second-ranking official of the United States Government require such repeated assurances that he had in mind no violation of the

> Constitution than it is comforting to have them at all. Of course, neither he nor any of his associates are advocating censorship—which would never survive judicial scrutiny. But it does not take overt censorship to cripple the free flow of ideas.

But it would have been foolish and self-deluding for us to have denied then, or for us to deny now, that the Vice President struck a responsive chord with many Americans. Many, many people out there made it clear that they thought that we got what was coming to us. As Chet Huntley said,

> [Agnew] knew clearly what he was doing. People were disturbed by adverse news, of course. What was the response from the government? "Let's get those guys," instead of trying to get rid of the aberrations and the disturbances.
>
> Agnew assembled a big pool of discontent, and there seems to be a willingness to delete many provisions of the Bill of Rights if need be.

Nor is this the time or the place to discuss in detail the substance of the points Agnew made. He was wrong—dead wrong—on most of his arguments. But insofar as he called for fairness, accuracy, and objectivity, insofar as he found fault with advocacy journalism, insofar as he suggested more searching *self*-examination by journalists, a greater self-recognition of our own fallibility, a more open receptivity to criticism, a less stubborn resistance to admitting error when error occurs—he was on sound ground. But he didn't invent those particular points on November 13 and 20. Many *within* the craft of journalism had been making these points long before and long after Agnew.

Those were *not* the crucial issues which Agnew's speech raised. Rather, there emerged the fundamental question of the propriety of Agnew's saying what he said—in the way he said it. The question—to turn Voltaire's statement on its head—was not whether one agreed with what he said, but his right to say it. Agnew was the second highest elected official in the land. He was, as we shall see, speaking for the President and the entire administration. And he was directing his fire in large part at *broadcasters,* whose relationship with the federal government is quite different than the relationship between the government and newspaper and news magazine publishers.

For, as Agnew took pains to point out, broadcasters are *licensed* and so are dependent for their very existence on the same federal government for whom Agnew spoke. The historical tension between government and printed press was always, and is, a tension between two reasonably equal contending forces. But—and there's the rub—when the highest officials of the federal government attack broadcast journalism, the game is unequal indeed. The government, through its licensing power, is *both* prosecutor *and* judge, and the guilty verdict is nothing less than capital punishment.

We shall see that the Nixon administration was fully aware of that. And so, inevitably, were broadcasters—the licensees.

But let me turn away from Vice President Agnew, and the grave implications of the very fact that *he,* as vice president, said what he said, to review what happened next.

First, we later learned, despite the initial White House disclaimers of any connection with the Agnew speeches, despite the assurances that Agnew was speaking for himself, that he was speaking for the administration and had been encouraged to do so by the White House. Indeed, the speeches had been written not by Agnew's staff, but by White House Special Assistant Patrick J. Buchanan. And Clark Mollenhoff, special counsel to President Nixon, later said that the speech "was developed by various White House aides." Mollenhoff added, "If you are asking me, does it reflect the administration's view, the evidence is abundant that it does." And, it was reported later, Nixon not only read a draft of Agnew's Des Moines speech but added his own sentences to it. It may have been the first, but it certainly was not the last time that earlier White House statements of alleged fact ultimately became "inoperative."

It was also clear that, among administration officials, Agnew had no monopoly on Agnewism. Immediately before and immediately after Agnew's speeches came these actions.

A member of the Subversive Activities Control Board and his wife made calls to television stations in Miami and Washington, D.C., asking for logs of their coverage of pro- and anti-Vietnam demonstrations. White House officials called stations around the country—licensees of the government—asking them whether they intended to editorialize on President Nixon's Vietnam policies and if so, what they planned to say. Dean Burch, the chairman of the FCC, the licensing authority, personally called the network company presidents, as well as a Phoenix station, asking for various transcripts relating to Vietnam—a chore normally left to a clerk calling another clerk. Burch made these calls the day after Nixon's November 3, 1969, Vietnam address, and three weeks after a memorandum from Jeb Magruder, special assistant to the president, to H. R. Haldeman, Nixon's chief of staff, in which Magruder proposed that as soon as Burch became chairman of the FCC—and by the time of the calls, he had—network news be monitored by the FCC. In his call to the president of CBS, Burch apologized for the request and explained that he was making it at the request of the White House. But the day after Agnew's Des Moines speech, Burch endorsed the Vice President's criticism of network news.

Herbert Klein, White House director of communications, said, on "Face The Nation," that if newspapers and networks do not "look at the problems they have today and if they fail to examine them, you do invite the government to come in."

And even Tricia Nixon chimed in. She told UPI that she had great admiration for Agnew's press critiques. She said she thought that Mr. Agnew had done a great deal of good because, she said, "you shouldn't underestimate the power of fear. They are afraid that if they don't shape up. . . ."

She didn't finish the sentence. She didn't have to.

The Nixon White House, and Agnew, made one thing perfectly clear—that among those falling the shortest in shaping up was the *Washington Post*. The Washington Post-Newsweek Company owned a television station in Miami, Florida. Just a few weeks after Agnew's Montgomery speech, a group of friends and former associates of President Nixon joined together to apply for the *Post* Miami station's license. That was the first time that happened to the *Post*. It wasn't the last.

Ultimately, the competing application for the Miami station was dropped and its license was renewed for the statutory three-year period—until 1972.

At the time, in late 1969, I was still unwilling to believe that all this was orchestrated. I wasn't certain that Agnew was Charlie McCarthy to the White House's Edgar Bergen. I thought that maybe, just maybe, Agnew, and the popular chord he obviously struck, made Agnewism contagious, and all these other administration officials just decided that this was a good bandwagon to get on. And so, when, on May 18, 1971, my colleague at CBS News, Walter Cronkite, made a speech in the course of which he said that "many of us see a clear indication on the part of this administration of a grand conspiracy to destroy the press," and that "the evidence today buttresses the suspicion that this administration has . . . conceived, planned, orchestrated, and is now conducting a program to reduce the effectiveness of a free press, and its prime target is television," I spoke to Walter about that—gently. I asked him whether that wasn't a little strong. Did he really *know* that there was "a grand conspiracy?" Did he really know, and not just suspect, that the administration had "conceived, planned, orchestrated, and was conducting" such a program?

As always, Walter was years ahead of me. It turned out that he was absolutely right. The only thing that Walter was wrong on—understandably, because no one in his right mind would have imagined that there were all those White House tapes and memoranda—was his statement that the charges he made in that remarkable speech could not be proved "short of uncovering documents which probably do not exist." The "documents" did exist and *were* uncovered in 1973 and 1974 in the House and Senate proceedings known as Watergate. And they established that, just as Walter had said, there *was* a "grand conspiracy" and that the administration has "conceived, planned, orchestrated a program to reduce the effectiveness of a free press, and its prime target" was television. Those documents also established how right Chet Huntley was when he had said in mid-1970 that "Nixon is playing the whole thing like a virtuoso. I have a feeling we haven't heard it all from him yet."

Because, as was said recently about something quite different, White House records "can teach those who do not remember and remind those who do," let me turn to what the memoranda and tapes showed. Indeed, we had not, as Chet had so accurately observed in 1970, "heard it all" from the White House "yet."

Chronologically, four extraordinary documents surfaced as the senate committee began its Watergate investigation. First, on October 17, 1969, just a few weeks before Agnew's Des Moines speech, Jeb Magruder wrote a memorandum to H. R. Haldeman. Its title—"The Shotgun versus the Rifle." Magruder attached to the memorandum a log of 21 separate requests which Nixon had made between September 16 and October 17 to individual members of the White House staff—Kissinger, Ehrlichman, Buchanan, Klein, Ziegler—that they take action concerning what Nixon regarded as unfavorable press stories or articles.

Six typical examples of Nixon's 21 requests: 1) to Klein and Ziegler—"President's request that you attack *Life* Magazine's editorial accusing the Administration of creating a coherence gap"; 2) to Klein—"President's request for letters to the editor regarding *Newsweek's* lead article covering the President's U.N. speech"; 3) to Klein—"President's request for a report on what action is taken concerning Senator Muskie's [sic] appearance on the 'Merv Griffin Show'"; 4) to Klein—"President's request that you demand equal time to counter John Chancellor's commentary regarding the Haynsworth nomination"; 5) to Klein (confidential)—"President's request that you take appropriate action to counter biased TV coverage of the Administration over the summer"; 6) confidential, to Peter Flanigan, assistant to the President—"President's request that you take action to counter Dan Rather's allegation that Hershey move was decided upon because of moratorium." And these were only six of the President's 21 orders over a one-month period.

Big brother sure was reading and watching!

Faced with this cascade of presidential requests, Magruder's memo to Haldeman began, "Yesterday you asked me to give you a talking paper on specific problems we've had in shot-

Agnew Plus Ten

Jeb Stuart Magruder testifying before the Ervin Committee in 1973.

gunning the media and anti-administration spokesmen on unfair coverage." The "talking paper" was intended to be used by Haldeman as a basis for discussion with the President. Magruder wrote that "this continual attempt to get to the media or to anti-administration spokesmen because of specific things they have said is very unfruitful and wasteful of our time." Magruder urged a broader approach "to get to this unfair coverage in such a way that we make a major impact on a basis which the networks, newspapers, and Congress will react to and begin to look at things somewhat differently." Magruder urged five different approaches. The first was "begin an official monitoring system" of television network news "through the FCC as soon as Dean Burch is officially on board as chairman." Another approach was the utilization of the antitrust weapon.

The second document uncovered in the course of the Watergate proceedings was a memorandum dated July 16, 1970,

Richard S. Salant

H. R. Haldeman testifying before the Senate Watergate Committee in 1973.

marked, in capital letters, "SECRET," from Larry Higby, Haldeman's assistant, to Jeb Magruder, special assistant to the President. The Higby memo was written right after *LIFE,* on the eve of Chet Huntley's retirement, quoted Chet as having said of President Nixon, "The shallowness of the man overwhelms me; the fact that he is president frightens me." Higby wrote to Magruder,

> We need to get some creative thinking going on an attack on Huntley for his statements in *LIFE.* One thought that comes to mind is getting all the people to sign a petition calling for the immediate removal of Huntley right now.
>
> The point behind this whole thing [Highby went on] is that we don't care about Huntley—he is going to leave anyway. What we are trying to do here is tear down the institution. Huntley will go out in a blaze of glory and we should attempt to pop his bubble. . . . Obviously, there are many things that we

can do, such as getting independent station owners to write NBC saying that they should remove Huntley now.

Let's put a full plan on this and get the thing moving. I'll contact Pat Buchanan and forward copies of my correspondence with him to you so that you will know what the Vice President is doing.

The third document was dated July 17, the very next day after Higby's memo, and marked, in capital letters, "CONFIDENTIAL/EYES ONLY." It was from the man to whom Higby had directed his memo, Jeb Magruder, and was addressed to Haldeman and Herbert Klein, White House director of communications. Its subject was "press objectivity." It was clearly designed to implement Higby's proposal to "tear down the institution." Here are some of Magruder's recommendations:

Mount a campaign, stimulated by Huntley's alleged statement, to "question" his "overall objectivity"—all in order "to cover the professional objectivity and ethics of the whole media." "Plant a column with a syndicated columnist which raises the question of objectivity and ethics in the news media . . . arrange for an article on the subject in a major consumer magazine"—a chore assigned to Klein. "Encourage the dean of a leading graduate school of journalism to publicly acknowledge that press objectivity is a serious problem"—to be assigned to Klein and Safire, special assistant to the President. "(A)rrange a seminar on press objectivity . . . [and] attempt to have this televised as a public service"—to be assigned to Klein. "(A)sk the Vice President to speak out on this issue"—Buchanan's assignment. "(H)ave Dean Burch [the chairman of the FCC] 'express concern' about press objectivity in response to a letter from a congressman. Produce a prime time special, sponsored by private funds, that would examine the question of objectivity and show how TV newsmen can structure the news by innuendo"—to be assigned to Klein and Magruder. "(H)ave outside groups petition the FCC"—to be the job of Charles Colson, special counsel to the President. "(H)ave a senator or congressman write a letter to the FCC suggesting the 'licensing' of individual newsmen, i.e. the airwaves belong to the public, therefore the public should be protected from the misuse of these airwaves by individual newsmen"—that to be attended to by Lyn Nofziger, deputy assistant to the President for congressional relations, and former press secretary to Ronald Reagan.

I don't know how many of these proposals ever ripened into action. It makes little difference. The memorandum was significant for what it showed about the mindset of the Nixon administration, and of its point man, Vice President Agnew. And it threw light on what had gone before, and what was still to come.

The fourth document was Charles Colson's September 25, 1970, "Eyes only, please" memorandum to Haldeman, giving Colson's boastful and somewhat questionable version of his visit to the heads of each of the three network companies. "They are very much afraid of us," he reported. "These meetings had a very salutary effect in letting them [the networks] know that we are determined to protect the President's position . . . and that we are not going to permit them to get away with anything that interferes with the President's ability to communicate. . . . We should take a very tough line, face to face, and other ways. . . . I will pursue with Dean Burch the possibility of an interpretive ruling by the FCC on the role of the President when he uses TV, as soon as we have a majority. I think that this point . . . would, of course, have an inhibiting impact on the networks." By "we," Colson meant the Nixon administration. The majority he was waiting for was a majority of the licensing authority—the FCC.

And then in May 1974 came the tapes and we saw what hardball the Nixon administration was playing during this earlier period, and who was playing it. The existence of the tapes had almost accidentally been disclosed—a reply by Alexander Butterfield, deputy assistant to President Nixon, to what probably was a chance shot-in-the-dark question by one of the minority counsel of the senate Watergate committee. After refusing, over and over again, to make these tapes, or the transcripts of them, available, Nixon finally did make them public. You may recall his television address—with all those volumes of transcripts behind him. That, he said, was all of it.

It wasn't all of it. Again, earlier White House statements became "inoperative." In the September 15, 1972, White House meeting among Haldeman, Dean, and Nixon, there was a notation that a portion of the transcript had been deleted because it did not relate to Watergate. What was excluded from the transcript was a discussion of the *Washington Post*—not a friendly discussion. But in May 1974, the transcript of that portion of the tape finally did become public. It went like this, right after the *Washington Post* and its Watergate reporting had been mentioned,

President: That's right. Right. The main thing is that the *Post* is going to have damnable, damnable problems out of this one. They have a television station.
Dean: That's right, they do.
President: And they're going to have to get it renewed.
Haldeman: They've got a radio station, too.
President: Does that come up too? The point is, when does it come up?
Dean: I don't know. But the practice of nonlicensees filing on top of licensees has certainly gotten more . . .
President: That's right.
Dean: . . . more active in the, this area.
President: And it's going to be goddam active here. (Dean laughs)
President: Well, the game has to be played awfully rough.

It certainly was. The *Washington Post* had not one, but two television licenses, one in Jacksonville, Florida, and one in Miami. Immediately after the 1972 election—just weeks after that September 15, 1972 conversation, when FCC license renewal time had come—applications were filed against both these *Post* Florida stations. There wasn't another challenge filed against any of the 44 stations in that area, except for those two. The two *Post* stations, it was widely recognized, were among the best in the nation. They had done superb investigative reporting, including the discovery and broadcast, after Carswell had been nominated by Nixon to the Supreme Court, of a white supremacist speech Carswell had made some years before.

Coincidentally—or not so coincidentally—as was the case with the competing application filed against the *Post's* Miami station in 1969, these 1972 competing applications were filed by people with ties to the administration. The president of the group which challenged the *Post's* Jacksonville license had been the Florida Finance Committee Chairman of President Nixon's reelection committee. A former counsel to the reelection committee had attended organizational meetings of the Jacksonville group which challenged the *Post* license. In Miami, the competing applicant was a company which included friends and business associates of President Nixon.

Ultimately, the competing applications were withdrawn and the *Post* licenses were renewed, but according to an affidavit filed with the FCC by Katharine Graham, the chairman of the Washington Post Company, there had been a drop in the price of the company's stock, a large increase in its legal fees, "(a) great burden in preparing to defend our past performance before the FCC, and unfortunate distractions of our officials and employees from the important business of operating their television stations."

Few things are, understandably, more distressing to a station licensee than the filing of a competing application against it at renewal time. Preparing to defend against competing applications, even if they never come to FCC hearing, can be an enormously expensive and time-consuming business. And the news of these competing applications sent shock waves among many broadcasters. To them, the implications were clear. They put the two of the *Washington Post's* reporting on Watergate and the two of the competing applications, and, very good at figures as they are, got four.

So those were some of the documents and the tapes. Permit me, now, to go back over this period from Agnew's Des Moines speech through 1974 to pick up on other episodes and activities which help fill in the outlines of the picture which has emerged to this point—the picture of what indeed was, as Cronkite had said, "A grand conspiracy to destroy the press." *Item:* The antitrust weapon against the networks. As we have seen on October 17, 1969, Jeb Magruder wrote a memo to Haldeman intended as a "talking paper" for Haldeman's discussion with President Nixon. That "shotgun versus rifle" memo proposed five strategies designed to "make impact on a basis which the networks, newspapers, and Congress will react and begin to look at things somewhat differently." One of those strategies to "achieve this goal" was "utilize the antitrust division to investigate various media relating to antitrust violations. Even the possible threat of antitrust action I think would be effective in changing their views." As we have noted, shortly thereafter, Agnew delivered his Des Moines and Montgomery speeches, warning of "the trend toward the monopolization of the great public information vehicles" and charging the networks with "monopoly." But the assistant attorney general in charge of the Department of Justice's antitrust division took no action, although he did pursue an active antitrust policy against other companies. This exasperated the President, and the transcript of an April 19, 1971, tape shows that the President told John Ehrlichman, "Get him [the assistant attorney general] out. In one hour . . . he is not going to stay one, uh, another minute. Not a minute. Because he's going after everybody, you know, just—why the hell don't he go after somebody that, uh." Ehrlichman laughed and said, "That's been suggested . . . your, uh, your television sense is apparently pretty good."

Finally, in April 1972, antitrust complaints against the networks were filed by the new acting attorney general, Richard Kleindienst. This, apparently, had slipped Buchanan's mind. A few weeks later, in a broadcast interview on May 4, 1972, he accused NBC News and CBS News of bias, and warned that television news programs might be the target of antitrust action if they continued "to freeze out opposing points of view and opposing information." And in November 1972, after a two-part report on the "CBS Evening News" about Watergate particularly enraged the White House, Charles Colson called

Frank Stanton, according to Stanton's sworn affidavit, and said, in substance, "You didn't play ball during the campaign. . . . We'll bring you to your knees in Wall Street and on Madison Avenue."

Item: NBC and Brinkley. On February 4, 1970, a Haldeman to Magruder memorandum, marked "confidential" and "high priority," expressed Haldeman's concern over a David Brinkley report on the federal budget, and NBC's treatment of the administration in general. "The need," Haldeman wrote, "probably is to concentrate on NBC and give some real thought as to how to handle the problem they have created. . . . I would like to see a plan from you . . . just some specific thinking on steps that can be taken to try to change this. . . . Get Klein and [Ron] Zeigler [White House press secretary] both involved in the thinking on this."

Item: Dan Rather and John Erlichman. On April 29, 1971, I joined John Ehrlichman for breakfast in New York City. I had never met Ehrlichman before. He had just been interviewed on the "CBS Morning News"; other CBS News people were present at the breakfast. In the midst of some small talk, Ehrlichman attacked Dan, whom he called a "hatchet man for the Democrats." He suggested that Dan be transferred back to Texas where he came from. PS—Dan wasn't. As I later state, Ehrlichman's suggestion assured that Dan would remain assigned to the White House for as long as Dan wanted.

Item: The Dan Schorr episode. Dan Schorr, the Watergate memos showed, was on the White House enemies list, characterized in a Colson memo as "a real media enemy." On August 18, 1971, he had broadcast a report on the "CBS Evening News" which particularly displeased the White House. The next day, he was summoned to the White House for a meeting with presidential assistant Pat Buchanan and others who complained to Dan about the piece, as they had also complained to CBS senior management. The following day—August 20—an FBI agent telephoned me at home. The FBI also called other CBS News people. As we learned later, in addition, the FBI called and questioned Dan's neighbors, friends and neighbors of his brother—a member of the faculty here at NYU. The FBI was investigating Dan, we were told, for an important job with the administration. Haldeman, it turned out, had requested a "background report" on Dan from the FBI. On March 22, 1973, Buchanan publicly stated that Schorr had never been offered—or had been considered for—any government job. In fact, Colson later testified in the Watergate proceedings that he and President Nixon had agreed on the cover story that Schorr was being considered for a federal job. And again, prior White House statements became "inoperative."

Item: PBS and Sandy Vanocur. On February 2, 1972, Clay Whitehead, director of the White House office of telecommunications, charged that public broadcasting often produced the kind of programming that "poses a great risk of thought control in the political process." Sander Vanocur, a public broadcasting correspondent, was particularly singled out for attack—he too was on the enemies list. A memo dated June 8, 1972, prepared by Pat Buchanan and subtitled "assault book," stated, "Given his performance the other night, Vanocur is a positive disaster for us. He may have to be fired or discredited if we are to get anything approaching an even shake out of that left-wing taxpayer-subsidized network." Soon, there were congressional outcries against Vanocur—both for his alleged biases *and* his salary level. And late in 1972, President Nixon vetoed public broadcasting's annual appropriation and reorganized its controlling board so as to replace the president of the corporation for public broadcasting with a man of his own choosing. Key personnel resigned, as a result, and the retiring chairman of the Public Broadcasting Service declared that the noncommercial network was virtually defunct as a source of critical reporting on national affairs.

Item: The break-ins. On April 9, 1972, there was a break-in at the Washington home of Dan Rather. He had returned home earlier than expected and found that his files had been ransacked. On July 9, and again on July 23, 1973, CBS News correspondent Marvin Kalb, on the enemies list, discovered his office at the State Department "in shambles with papers strewn around." He had been among the four newsmen ordered to be wiretapped by the FBI beginning in May 1969. On August 22,

1973, ABC disclosed that "sensitive" papers and tapes relating to aspects of the Watergate case were stolen in a burglary of ABC's Washington News Bureau.

Item: The White House and the affiliates. Networks, as most of you know, may own only five VHF and two UHF television stations. The remaining 200 or so television stations around the country which are affiliated with each network are separately and independently owned. Those affiliates are free to broadcast, or not broadcast, any and all network programs. Networks may not, under the law, *require* any affiliate to carry any program. In this sense, affiliates are like a faucet—unless the manager of an affiliate decides to turn on the faucet, the network program never reaches the public in the affiliate's area. Without affiliates, there is no network. And the White House, clearly, knew and exploited this. What it could not accomplish directly against the networks, it sought to accomplish through the networks' affiliates.

Thus, as we have seen, Higby's July 16, 1970, memorandum suggesting administration actions to exploit the Huntley episode, proposed, among other things, "getting independent stations [that is, affiliates] to write NBC saying that they should remove Huntley now." Fred Friendly stated in 1970 that Herb Klein "told a CBS station owner, 'You fellows do an excellent job. Why do you rely on CBS?'" In a speech to NBC television affiliates in May 1972, Ronald Reagan said that he was convinced that there was bias in network news, and he urged the station managers to prevent this bias from occurring. He said, "if someone down the line is slanting things, you are not neutral simply because you keep your hands off. . . . If you are unable to find a way to use your influence to police the irresponsible broadcaster, you may not have any industry left to police—at least, not the independent, private commercial system we know today."

And then Clay Whitehead, the director of the White House office of telecommunications, picking up on Reagan's cue, put it all together. On December 18, 1972, he made a speech in Indianapolis—a speech which, despite earlier denials, he later testified had been cleared by the White House. "It represented the administration viewpoint," he testified. It was a classic stick and carrot gambit, in which he offered stations the dearly hoped for longer license periods, *if* they policed the network news. He charged that the broadcasters had failed to guarantee "reasonable, realistic, and practical opportunities for the presentation and discussion of conflicting views on controversial issues." He said that "the station owners and managers cannot abdicate responsibility for news judgment." He urged them to take action against "ideological plugola" in news. The networks, he charged, had demonstrated their inability to guard against such "plugola" and so it was up to the affiliates—the licensees—to do so.

To assure this, he proposed legislation, to be drafted in the White House, which would emphasize the station owner's total responsibility for what his station broadcasts from a network, and would hold the station owner responsible for seeing to it that wherever a program might originate, it must conform to *local* standards of taste and political outlook. Whitehead said, "station managers . . . who fail to correct imbalance or consistent bias from the networks, or who acquiesce by silence, can only be considered willing participants to be held fully accountable [by the broadcaster's community at license renewal time]." If the station assumed, and properly carried out, that obligation, the license would be renewed for five years—instead of three years, and if the FCC should decide that a station failed to do that, its license would not be renewed—and the broadcaster would be out of business.

Item: A personal note on the administration and the affiliates. The Nixon administration was, as noted, immensely displeased with the networks' reporting of the Indochina war, and of the divisions and demonstrations in this country. Indeed, that was a major thrust, and the genesis, of Agnew's November 13 Des Moines speech. In 1970, a delegation of CBS television network affiliates came to New York to tell me how much they disliked our reporting. They proposed to go to Vietnam—with or without me—to talk directly to our reporters there, and tell them what a biased, inaccurate, and unpatriotic job they were doing. For two days, we discussed and argued. They finally abandoned the idea. But when I told the chief proponent among the delegation that I regarded the proposal as an atrocious interference with our reporters in Vietnam, he told me that it had not been his idea. Rather, he said, another affiliate who wasn't at our meeting had made the proposal, and that other affiliate, he told me, had broached the idea after he had been at a meeting at the White House where he had been asked whether he wasn't unhappy about the CBS News Vietnam coverage. When he said he was, a White House official—I never found out who—suggested that the affiliate do something about it—by forming a delegation of affiliates to go to Vietnam to tell our reporters of their unhappiness.

One more item, on a lighter note. A personal, long-distance confrontation Vice President Agnew and I had in a phantom exchange of Christmas gifts. Agnew had made a number of speeches critical of "CBS Reports: The Selling of The Pentagon," broadcast in 1971. He made public a list of Christmas presents he was giving. For me, he listed "A news desk with legs cut on the bias so that the documentaries will come out straight." I regret to report that I never received it; it would have made a nice souvenir. But when a reporter asked me what *my* gift to the Vice President would be, I asked, "What can you give a man who has nothing?" *He* never got that, either.

And so, what does all this come down to? After all, presidents—Washington, John Adams, Jefferson, Wilson, Franklin D. Roosevelt, Truman, Kennedy, Johnson—had, at some time or another during their incumbencies, very unkind things to say about the press. I expect that if one really dug into history, one would find that, with a single exception, every president has let loose at the press—we are, after all, watchdogs and we are ornery and exasperating. The exception? William Henry Harrison, inaugurated March 4, 1841. He died exactly one month later, April 4, 1841, before the customary—indeed obligatory—honeymoon between a president and the press was over.

No. What made the Agnew attacks so different, so threatening, was that, as the recital of all this clearly establishes, he was speaking for the President and the administration. This wasn't aberrant, occasional scatter-shot. It was, precisely as Chet Huntley and Walter Cronkite had said, a grand conspiracy, orchestrated by the President and enthusiastically played out by an entire administration. These were men who believed in speaking loudly—*and* in carrying a very big stick.

Why? As I have noted, it seems reasonable to infer that Nixon recognized early on that first, because of Vietnam, and later, because of Watergate, his power, the realization of his objectives, might well be, and were being, frustrated by the press, whose historical function and responsibility properly to perform, which the First Amendment included in the Constitution, had to be neutralized. That recognition by the Nixon administration was what Agnew, and all that went with Agnewism, was all about. And that is what made it all so ominous, so important. The tragic, ugly campaign went to the heart of the independence of the press, and its fulfillment of its role in a democracy. Earlier skirmishes between presidents and the press had been occasional, spasmodic, but this was a systematic all-out war waged by the administration. And as I have noted, as far as television news was concerned, it was a war in the waging of which no president used the ultimate weapon which the Nixon administration proposed to use—the weapon of licenses, the power to put a broadcaster out of business.

What it all demonstrated—and what must be of deep concern to everyone who believes in a free press as a cornerstone of a viable democracy—was the vulnerability of the press, and especially of that part of the press which is broadcast journalism on which, for good or ill, a large majority of Americans rely as their primary source of news, and one-third as their *sole* source of news.

What emerged, during this black period, is what Alexander Hamilton had pointed out when he opposed the adoption of a press freedom guarantee in the First Amendment as futile:

> What signifies a declaration [he wrote] that the liberty of the press shall be inviolably preserved? What is the liberty of the press? Who can give it any definition that would not leave the utmost latitude for evasion? I hold it to be impracticable; and from that I infer that its security, whatever fine declarations may

be inserted in any constitution respecting it, must altogether depend on public opinion, and on the general spirit of the people and of the government.

I am mighty glad that Hamilton's argument did not prevail and that the First Amendment did forbid any abridgment of a free press. But how prescient Hamilton was. If my recital shows anything, it establishes how "the general spirit . . . of the government" during this period from 1969 to 1974, could subvert press freedom. And so can "the general spirit of the people." Tragically, too many people hold no great affection for, or understanding of, the First Amendment's guarantee of a free press. Too often, they look upon the press' invocation of the First Amendment like a witness claiming the Fifth. Many letters came to me during this period, supporting Nixon and Agnew, and demanding we be forced to shut up. This was typical of hundreds—a letter addressed to Dean Burch, copies to Agnew and me:

> Dear Mr. Chairman:
> I hope that you will make the greatest effort in your life to have some federal legislation passed whereby the TV networks will have "free speech" [in quotes] taken from them. The time is far past when they should be censored with all the power that the federal government can muster. . . . Let us stop this by taking away from the networks that precious privilege of free speech—they absolutely do not deserve it. Therefore, let's get busy.

Only the fair deserve the First Amendment, so the sentiment goes, and who and what is fair depends on the eye of the beholder. If a viewpoint or fact is agreeable and palatable, you're allowed to say it, print it, broadcast it. But if it's disagreeable and unpalatable, then it's not freedom, but impermissible license, unprotected by the Constitution.

Some years ago, CBS News had a public opinion survey conducted for a "60 Minutes" broadcast on the Bill of Rights, including the guarantee of free speech and a free press. Among other questions which were asked was "except in time of war, do you think newspapers, radio, and television should have the right to report any story, even if the government feels it is harmful to our national interest?" Fifty-five percent said they should not have any such right; only 42 percent said they should.

Small wonder that Agnew and the Nixon administration had no great concern that there might be a popular revulsion at what they were trying to do, and did, to the press.

And we have seen tonight that there were two more areas of the gravest vulnerabilities for broadcast journalism. One is the vulnerability arising from the special structure of a network— its dependence on its affiliates to reach the public at all. The second is the even greater—and more direct, omnipresent and pervasive—fact that the broadcast news is part of broadcasting, and so there must be a government-granted license, renewable every three years. No license, no broadcast news.

Since John Milton, it has been a given that a government-licensed press cannot be a free press, and a press is not free it if is subject to government license. But broadcast journalism *is* subject to license. In the litany to which I have subjected you this evening, you have seen how Agnew, and the Nixon Administration, with their instincts for the jugular, exploited these two grave vulnerabilities. They knew exactly what they were doing. The miracle—and it is nothing less than that—is that we somehow survived, intact, I believe, with our flags flying. As Jeff Greenfield noted a few weeks ago in the CBS News broadcast "Sunday Morning," in observing the anniversary of Agnew's Des Moines speech:

> The clearest effect of the Agnew speech and confrontation it heralded was to underscore the fragile nature of broadcast journalism's independence. A network may appear very powerful to those it's analyzing, but among station licenses, affiliate pressures, government regulation, sponsor concerns, it's sometimes remarkable that anything of substance gets on the air at all. And when a president decides to go after broadcast news for political reasons, he's going after a very vulnerable institution.

There's no easy solution. There have to be licenses, and the Congress, and the public, do not seem to be ready to forbid the FCC to consider news content in granting, renewing, or revoking licenses. Nor, as the Supreme Court demonstrated in its last term, is the court ready to withdraw from its *Red Lion* decision that broadcast journalism has significantly lesser free press rights than print.

Wiser and more objective heads than ours must, some day, find a way out—find a way to reconcile the irresistible force of press freedom with the immovable object of licensing. For we cannot really be sure that Agnew and Nixon were what the broadcast schedulers call a special broadcast: "OTO"—one time only. None of us knows whether it *will* happen again. But next time, the nation, and the press and the network news, may not be so lucky. Next time, a different administration may be more subtle, less overt, less inept than were Agnew and Nixon and their associates. Next time, all those accidents which I have reviewed may not happen again to save us.

The time to find solutions, the time to fight for liberty, is now, while we still have it. Meanwhile, the best we in broadcast journalism can do is uncompromisingly to follow Elmer Davis' advice: "Don't let the bastards scare you."

And so, ten years and two days after Des Moines, let me repeat what Jeff Greenfield said at the end of his broadcast marking that occasion: "Happy Anniversary."

And, I would add, "While we still can celebrate it."

2

The Press and the Presidency

November 13, 1980

Perspective

Long considered one of the most powerful of American institutions, the press has been called "the fourth branch of government." Perhaps the most telling aspect of the press' political significance is its relationship with the president. As the second speaker in the Chet Huntley Memorial Lecture Series, two-time Pulitzer Prize-winning journalist Anthony Lewis discusses the evolution of this important and dynamic relationship. He argues that, despite sincere efforts by most media representatives to give fair, accurate, and balanced coverage of the presidency and let the public decide how to think about the issues, the press does indeed have a great effect on public sentiment towards the president and the election process.

Particularly in recent years, with the advent of radio and television, the press and the presidency have become tightly entwined—though not always happily so. With the limited time granted to news broadcasts on many television and radio stations, the decision-making process of what—and who—gets coverage has become increasingly important. As Lewis points out, the question for press representatives is often less "Do we like it?" than "Is it news?" But, in making such a judgment, the press can tip the balance. Particularly in a presidential campaign, the amount of coverage a given candidate receives has much to do with his or her skill in dealing with the press. The press, Lewis contends, bears great responsibility to the public for this reason.

In the past, political party bosses made decisions on who would run for office, but with the factionalization of major parties and the spread of primary elections, this process has become far less cohesive. In addition, radio and television have made candidates more visible to the public. The press, by determining who and what to cover in a news broadcast, is now largely responsible for determining which candidates are presented to the voter and what kind of information the voter acquires about the candidates. Anthony Lewis believes that journalists should recognize the powerful position they hold and become tougher on candidates and officeholders alike. Dan Rather was noted, for instance, for his tough stance during interactions with Richard Nixon. And although many applauded him for this, he was also accused of disrespect for the office of the president. During one noted press conference at the time of the Watergate investigation, Rather was greeted with a mixture of applause and boos as he rose to ask a question. Nixon inquired as to whether Rather was "running for something." To which Rather replied, "No, sir. Are you?"

But there is a clear distinction between disrespect for the office of the president and perceptive, hard-headed questioning on substantive issues. Sam Donaldson of ABC News once asked Jimmy Carter near the end of his administration, "Do you recognize that there is a charge of incompetence that settles over you?" Although such tactics often create an uncomfortable tension, they also give the official an opportunity to respond to the sort of blunt questions that are being asked by the public.

Lewis recommends that the press adopt a more balanced stance. Although it is vital for journalists to broach the most significant issues of the day when they speak with the president, it is equally necessary that they show due respect for the office. Anthony Lewis suggests "less scandal," of the sort that ruined such candidates as Gary Hart in the past, and "more analysis." He hopes that the press will probe into issues that truly matter—economic, social, and political problems that may be less interesting than Al Gore's alleged marijuana use, but in the long run are far more important to the American public in arriving at a well thought-out decision about a given candidate. Presidents and presidential candidates need the press, just as the press needs them, to make news. As Lewis notes, the two are "locked in a deadly embrace." It is not an "embrace" that either side can break, but it can, Lewis convincingly asserts, be handled more effectively by both the president and the press; the result would be a better informed voter and a more responsible president.

The Press and the Presidency

Introduction of Anthony Lewis by John Chancellor

> John Chancellor has long been a respected name in broadcast journalism and was a member of the selection committee for this lecture series. He has served since 1982 as a commentator for the "NBC Nightly News," and has been at the center of the field since the late 1950s, winning numerous journalism awards. Chancellor introduced the second speaker in the Chet Huntley Memorial Lecture Series, author and newspaper columnist Anthony Lewis.

Introduction

*I*t's a pleasure to introduce Anthony Lewis. I've admired his work for many years, and I think the world is a better place because of his writing.

After Harvard, he joined the staff of the "News of the Week in Review" at the *New York Times,* and after some time there, a personage at the *Times* told him he did not have a future at the paper. So Tony Lewis left the *Times,* ended up on general assignment for the *Washington Daily News,* and three years later, won the Pulitzer Prize.

That triumph was made sweeter by the fact that before he won the prize, his work had been noticed by James Reston. There's a legend that Scotty Reston was telling his superiors at the *Times* that they should hire (or rehire) Tony Lewis, when a copy clerk brought in the AP bulletin that Tony Lewis had won the Pulitzer Prize. We think that may have helped.

I've deliberately not tried to check that story, because I like it so much. In any case, the *Times* did hire him back, and thus continued a notable career—Neiman Fellow at Harvard, where he studied law; a second Pulitzer in 1963, for his coverage of the Supreme Court; his wonderful book, *Gideon's Trumpet;* seven sweet years as chief of the London bureau; his own column; a gracious residency in Cambridge, Massachusetts; a lectureship at the Harvard Law School; and a mandate to travel and teach and write and think.

It has involved a lot of hard work, and it hasn't all been easy. A good journalist ought to take stands, and he has. Taking stands means taking criticism, and Tony Lewis has had his share of that. What I find most appealing about him is a quality of what we might call a kind of fierce goodness, a kind of militant decency, which has distinguished his life and his work.

Anthony Lewis

Born March 27, 1927, in New York City, Lewis went from Harvard University to the Sunday desk at the New York Times *(1948–52). It was at the Washington Daily News, however, that he won in 1955 the Heywood Broun Memorial Award and a Pulitzer Prize in national reporting for a series of articles on the unwarranted discharge of a civilian employee of the U.S. Navy. In 1955 he returned to the* Times, *serving at the Washington bureau (1955–64), as the London bureau chief (1965–72), and as an editorial columnist (1969-). A Nieman Fellow (1956–57) and, for 15 years, a lecturer in law at Harvard University, Lewis won a second Pulitzer Prize in 1963. He is the author of several books, including* Gideon's Trumpet *(1964), the story of a Florida prisoner's Supreme Court battle for justice, and* Make No Law: The Sullivan Case and the First Amendment *(1991), a historical account of the landmark trial over the issue of press freedom. Lewis currently serves as James Madison Visiting Professor at Columbia University.*

The Press and the Presidency

I did not know Chet Huntley, and so I cannot add to the personal tribute given by Richard Salant in the brilliant lecture that opened this series. But for me, as for so many others, Chet Huntley helped to inaugurate a new relationship between the press and public affairs. (I use that old-fashioned word, press, in preference to the vogue word, media, because it somehow sounds less pretentious.) The model of television news created by Huntley and his colleagues a generation ago—it is that long now—changed the role of the press in this country, or at least began the process of change. Journalists became more visible: broadcast journalists especially, of course, but not only them. Political writers as well as the anchormen and reporters on television became in a significant sense actors in the American political drama.

Most of us in the press feel uncomfortable when we are described as part of the political system. We prefer, for good reasons, to think of ourselves as outsiders—and we remain outsiders in a formal, legal, constitutional sense. But there is no use pretending that the press has no effect on how the system works, or in trying to shrug off responsibility. If Americans are discontented with their political system, and they are, some introspection is in order on the part of all those involved, including the press.

I am going to talk this evening about the relationship that has changed most dramatically in my lifetime: that between the press and the presidency. It is a large subject, and one on which I have only started to educate myself. My thoughts are tentative, my expertise nonexistent. But in preparing this talk I found that a good many others, politicians and political scientists among them, have reflected on the subject, and I shall draw on their thoughts. I am going to talk about two phases of press effect on the presidency: electing and governing.

The public tends to believe that the press is biased in favor of one side or another in presidential campaigns. A study published recently by the Public Agenda Foundation included a large-scale poll of public attitudes toward newspapers and broadcasters; it showed an overwhelming majority in favor of laws requiring "fairness" by all press institutions toward candidates and issues. For example, 82 percent of those surveyed said there should be a law making newspapers give each major party candidate exactly the same amount of coverage. That is an unconvincing solution. What coverage an event gets has to depend on someone's judgment, and I would rather see editors make that judgment than some official appointed to supervise the press. Not only do I prefer it, the Constitution does. The Supreme Court is not always a predictable institution, but I think this is a certainty: if there ever was a law requiring newspapers to give exactly the same amount or kind of coverage to candidates A and B, the Court would hold it unconstitutional. That is because the First Amendment keeps officials out of the business of editing. As Chief Justice Burger put it in one case, "Editing is what editors are for."

(The Broadcasters in this room are no doubt thinking that on the question of enforced political "fairness" they are less equal than others in the press. The Supreme Court has allowed just such a rule to be enforced on broadcasting, the First Amendment notwithstanding. All I can say is that the justification for that unequal treatment, if it ever existed, has vanished. Broadcasting could be thus regulated, the Court said, because the number of channels was limited. In fact, now, most American have access to far more television and radio stations than newspapers. How much of a choice that gives them is a different question. But perhaps the Gresham's Law of broadcasting will be amended by multiple cable channels.)

All that is an aside. The important thing about the reported public desire for a law against unequal newspaper coverage of campaigns is that it is a solution to a nonexistent problem. Yes, there is some bias in journalism. But conscious manipulation of political stories to help one candidate or another is not common nowadays, certainly not on the major newspapers or television news programs. I am talking about news reports. Editorials and columns are different; opinions are expected there. But they do not generally infect the news columns. In the election we have just had, for example, the *Wall Street Journal's* editorial page gave unflagging support to Governor Reagan, sounding a little worried only when he grew soft on such dubious liberal enterprises as loans to the Chrysler Corporation, but in the news columns of the *Journal* one found searching reports and analyses on Governor Reagan, his ideas, and his advisers. The point is obvious. In most of the American press the Colonel McCormick school of journalism is out of fashion. News stories no longer tell the reader to vote for the candidate who will keep King George out of Chicago.

The problem is a different one. In the interminable process that we now use to elect a president, the press decides what is news—and who is news. Not good news or bad, whether we like it or not, just "Is it news?" And that seemingly straightforward judgment—just the facts, Ma'am—has large consequences.

Consider the rise of Jimmy Carter. Do you remember how it happened? Back in 1975 he was an unknown former governor of Georgia who wandered around the country telling anyone who would listen, "My name is Jimmy Carter, and I'm running for president." Then, while nobody was looking, he spent a lot of time in Iowa, made friends, convinced some Democrats of his merits and finished first in the Democratic caucuses in January 1976. He got 29 percent of the delegates—not a majority, but more than anyone else. That was not so important in itself. What mattered was that Johnny Apple of the *New York Times* wrote a story saying Jimmy Carter's surprise victory made him a serious candidate for the Democratic nomination. Others, in particular the television networks, began treating him as a serious candidate. And the rest is history. Well, not quite. Carter had to do a few more things before he could appear at the Democratic convention and say, "My name is Jimmy Carter, and I'm running for President;" and then he had to do some more before he staggered across the finish line in November, barely first. Of course I have greatly oversimplified. But I do believe that the crucial step came in Iowa in January, 1976. That was when he was described in the *New York Times* as a serious candidate.

What the press did in that instance, to give it a quasi-academic sound, was to perform a legitimizing function. It anointed Jimmy Carter. It told the voters that they could be for him and not be eccentric—not just the people of his own state or the South, but of New Hampshire and Pennsylvania and Ohio. He was a serious candidate.

Or take the case of John Anderson in this election, a candidate almost wholly created by the press. We found him different, iconoclastic, a figure of interest in what we considered a dull group of Republican primary candidates. David Broder said reporters liked John Anderson for many of the same reasons we liked Eugene McCarthy: "He uses language well, and language is our coin of exchange. He says what he othinks, as we like to think we do. He can be caustically critical of other politicians, which is our stock in trade." And, Broder added, "We tend to overlook the moral arrogance implicit in many of his judgments, because we have more than our share of that quality ourselves."

So the press made John Anderson a hero in the primary stage. He never won a primary, but he was painted as a brave battler against the odds. I contributed a bit of the Glo-coat myself. And when he became an independent candidate, the press continued to take him seriously, far more seriously, in my judgment, than anything but the size of his ego could justify. David Broder warned Anderson about the ego business in a column last March. Don't follow the pattern of Gene McCarthy, he said, whose "self-righteous anger at the party's rejection of his candidacy made him a divisive and destructive force." Remember, he said to Anderson, "those are papier-mâché haloes, not real ones." But Anderson did not remember. And I think the press had some responsibility for the haloes.

John Anderson on the campaign trail in Miami in 1980.

I do not want to sound cynical, because I am not. In a country this size someone has to perform the function of framing the choices for the mass of citizens to make. The United States cannot operate on some scheme of direct democracy as in ancient Athens, with every citizen standing in the town square and raising a hand—and even in Athens citizenship was restricted by sex and status. In practice, Americans have to choose their president from a limited number of possibilities presented to them. And if the press today is helping to frame those choices to announce the legitimate alternatives—that is because other methods have atrophied.

In the old days the preliminary selection was made by political parties and their leaders—that is, the bosses. The parties in each state, under the influence of leaders, picked most of the delegates to the national convention. And there the candidates were chosen by a process of compromise and deals. Just to use that word, deals, tells you that we are talking about the Bad Old Days. To give you an example, Franklin D. Roosevelt was nominated by a deal. He did not have enough votes to win at the 1932 convention, so his backers made a deal to put John Nance Garner of Texas on the ticket as his running mate. Garner was a crusty old character who is best remembered today for having said that the vice presidency was not worth a bucket of warm spit. As I said, the Bad Old Days.

As you know, those days were ended by the reform movement in the Democratic party. It began as a reaction to the disaster of the 1968 convention, when millions watching television saw hatred in the Chicago convention hall and brutal police tactics against demonstrators outside. After that, the Democrats decided that they wanted a nominating process controlled by the people instead of the bosses. They persuaded more and more states to adopt binding primaries for the choice of national convention delegates. As a result, the number of delegates chosen by state and local leaders dropped from 75 percent of the total number at the Democratic convention in 1968 to about 25 percent this year. The full-time politicians were practically driven out. If you went to Madison Square Garden last summer, you know that many of the familiar Democratic faces were missing.

So the people now choose the party nominee by voting in small numbers, significantly in small states, for delegates bound to a particular candidate. But as I say, Athenian democracy would not work in this country. Someone had to fill the role that the bosses used to play, of narrowing down the possibilities to a point where the voters could choose. And that turned out to be the press.

Professor James David Barber of Duke University, one of our leading students of the presidency, put it in his recent book that new elites "take over the work of identifying, winnowing, advancing, and publicizing candidates for President. With the lapse of the parties, the people turn to their newspapers and

The Press and the Presidency

Chicago police attempt to disperse demonstrators outside the Conrad Hilton, Democratic National Convention headquarters hotel. The picture was taken by freelance photographer Michael Boyer.

magazines and television sets for guidance. And it is there, in political journalism, that they find a new elite who, through no conscious conspiracy or neurotic lust for power, have had power thrust upon them."

The new reality was quickly grasped by the candidates. Professor Barber says: "The primary task a presidential candidate faces today is not building a coalition of organized interests, or developing alliances with other candidates or politicians in his party, or even winning over the voters whose hands he shakes. If he has his modern priorities straight, he is first and foremost a seeker after favorable notice from the journalists who can make or break his progress."

That is a pretty exalted role—"the new powerbroker," Professor Barber calls the political journalist, "filling the gap vacated by yesterday's bosses. There he stands, between people and President. Whether he knows it or not, the impressions he composes and conveys are now the blood of presidential politics."

The question is how well it works. Well, instead of Franklin Roosevelt and Jack Garner, the reformed nominating system has given us George McGovern and Jimmy Carter and Ronald Reagan. I do not want to be unfair, to those three men or to the system. After all, the old convention bargaining process did not only produce F.D.R. It also gave us Franklin Pierce and Warren G. Harding. And after 103 ballots at the old Madison Square Garden in 1924—imagine that on television for a week!—it gave the Democrats John W. Davis. But without being unfair, I think we can identify one fault in the new system. That is the reluctance of those who have taken over the winnowing and legitimizing function from the parties, namely the press, to make judgments on the wisdom and ability of the candidates. It is a paradoxical fault. The very effort of the political writers to be detached, to withhold personal reactions, removes a necessary element of judgment from the system. At least that is the view of an expert witness I now call. He is a man who, as Oscar Wilde said in a different context, has risen from the ranks of the aristocracy.

John Sears, who was Ronald Reagan's campaign manager until he was fired in New Hampshire, has now made it to the status of newspaper columnist. And this is what he has told his new colleagues in the press about their role in the election process:

> They did not ask for the responsibility of picking the candidates and deciding which of the survivors should be the President. But it is undeniably theirs. With the disintegration of strong political parties . . . the voters have nowhere else to turn for advice. Thus . . . by not qualifying the reporting of a man's successes in an early caucus or primary by the political realities that surround it, and . . . by not informing the voters what these

men who run for President are really like, the media substantially alter what would otherwise be the result.

What does John Sears mean when he says the press does not tell the voters what these candidates are really like? He explains that he wants us to "ask the hard questions and make the harsh observations." And he is not shy about giving examples of what he means by harsh observations. Writing in the *Washington Journalism Review* in September, he said John Chancellor "could ask Jimmy Carter about the economy, and when Carter says he is sure it's getting better, Chancellor should say: 'You must be an absolute fool or a liar.'" He had a suggestion, too, for Jack Germond, the tough political columnist of the *Washington Star*. He might ask Governor Reagan "how he expects to deal with the energy problem and when Ron says he is sure there is plenty of oil in the United States if we would just get the government out of the way and let the old free enterprise system go to work, Germond should say 'Governor, that's the most asinine thing I've ever heard a presidential candidate say in the thirty years I've been covering national politics.'"

You may doubt that Mr. Sears was serious in those suggestions. But his point was really that journalists are *not* going to talk that way to candidates—and that somebody should. Indeed, he said the candidates used to hear comments just that tough from the people who did the winnowing in the old days, the political leaders. By way of example, he quoted some things he actually heard politicians say to Richard Nixon in 1968.

One was "Dick, if you don't really have any solution to Vietnam, why don't you say so instead of boring me with all this garbage?" *I* have to admit, that is more interesting than the conversations I have with politicians, or the ones I overhear other journalists having with them. Most of us are too polite, or just too timid, to talk that way. Yes, columnists give their opinions, and sometimes they are strong: No more Mr. Nice Guy. But the political reporters who work at the heart of the process—the David Broders and Jack Germonds—

The Jimmy Carter-Ronald Reagan presidential debate of 1980.

customarily do not. And neither do the television anchormen and reporters who give most Americans most of their political information. Because to do so would be to show "bias." Just the facts—no judgments.

I should say just a word about a familiar concern: the power of television as a medium. Just after the Iowa caucuses, it is said, Governor Reagan was looking for a way to recover from his defeat there. He needed to do something that would command attention. Someone suggested that when he went on "60 Minutes," as he was scheduled to do, he propose a blockade of Cuba as a response to the Soviet invasion of Afghanistan. And he did. So the availability of the medium evoked a hyperbolic message. Candidates have always looked for dramatic gestures, but television does raise the stakes.

The Carter-Reagan debate is an even more immediate example of the intensifying effect of television. The experts all seem agreed now that a challenger gains in a presidential debate for merely being there—from appearing in the ring with the incumbent. Campaigns always gave the challenger a chance to make himself known to the electorate, to reassure the voters, to seem less of an unknown, a risk. But a television debate can do that, powerfully, in a few hours.

Then there is the way television has affected the mechanical conduct of campaigns. I was following President Carter when he went to a small Knights of Columbus hall in Gloucester City, N.J., and talked for an hour with 50 people: Jim Rafferty, a bricklayer, his family, and friends. In the last century 100,000 voters gathered in a field and listened to William Jennings Bryan bellow at them, without benefit of electronics, about the cross of gold. Today 50 people meet the president of the United States for a quiet talk and millions listen, thanks to television. Or do they?

Of course there is exaggeration in all this. John Sears and James David Barber and others sometimes give the impression that the press leads the public around by the nose in today's election process, and I do not think that is true. John Connally spent $12 million in the primaries, and entertained reporters at his ranch, and had plenty of media impact. But the public did not want him. And in the general election campaign all those carefully created media events and all the print and broadcast advertising did not make the difference in the end. To a large extent issues made the difference, or so I believe. For both domestic and foreign reasons American public opinion had moved decisively to the right. People were frightened of a continuing inflation that they connected with liberal government spending programs. They were frustrated at the loss of American power abroad, at the sense of impotence symbolized by the hostages in Iran. Those underlying themes were reflected in dozens of specific issues, from taxation to arms control. Disappointment with Jimmy Carter as president was a factor. But I think the tremendous swing in the Senate shows that something much deeper was involved. This was an issue election to a greater extent than American elections usually are.

I think the press can be faulted for not giving sufficient weight to the issues in election coverage. Through much of

1980 I felt that I was reading and hearing and seeing more about the manner of politics than the matter. In the primaries we heard all about momentum and gaffes and tactics. In the general election we had Reagan's fumbles and Carter's mean streak. And all along we had the Who's Ahead stories. The *Washington Journalism Review* studied the coverage in three newspapers during the primaries—the *New York Times,* the *Washington Post* and the *Chicago Tribune*—and concluded that "the press was obsessed with predicting what would happen and who was ahead." According to its survey, the *Post* ran more than five times as many stories on the horse race—that is, who's ahead—as on issues; the *Times* and *Tribune* ran nearly twice as many. It is only fair to add that toward the end of the general election campaign, especially, there were serious and valuable pieces on issues.

We are all sophisticated enough in the press now to be aware of our imperfections, in covering the presidential election process as in other things. We may also be getting used to critical examination from outside. Tim Crouse ended the romantic era when he wrote about "The Boys on the Bus"—the McGovern campaign bus. The journalism reviews examine the entrails every month now, and there are press commentators in other magazines and papers. So we can look forward to more extended discussions of the performance of newspapers and broadcasters in the 1980 campaigns. I hope the press critics and the political scientists ask for more attention to issues and less to the sporting side of elections. I hope and believe the press can provide a deeper level of analysis.

But I have to say that I see no ready solution to the central dilemma I have mentioned: the press' limited ability to perform the function it has inherited form the political leaders of old, that of framing the decisions for the voters. I am pessimistic about that because it is not just a press problem; it is far larger, and more troubling.

John Sears is just teasing, I think, when he calls on the press to be rough and nasty and judgmental. His real aim is to get back to the old system, where the mediators between the people and the candidates were politicians. "If the media decide in their wisdom that they do not want to make these decisions," he says, "they do not really want to tell us what they think of these men, they are . . . too embarrassed to ask the tough questions, please help us poor politicians to get our business back."

I do not think they will get the old business back, at least not in the same form. Those who are nostalgic for the smoke-filled room will have to go to a movie: Sunrise at Madison Square Garden, that sort of thing. And I say that not because the press wants to hold on to its role as "the new powerbroker," in Professor Barber's phrase. Far from it. Most political reporters are uncomfortable when they read a professorial analysis of their influence.

No, the reason we cannot go back to where we were in 1932 is that the basis of parties as it existed then has disappeared. The Poor American does not go to his Tammany Hall district leader for a scuttle filled with coal or a Thanksgiving basket of food. He goes to a social worker paid by the federal government, or to a counter where he gets his food stamps. The kinds of human dependencies that knit local party structures together no longer exist.

We have never had in the United States the strong, centralized, ideologically unified parties familiar in European countries. Our national parties have been loose coalitions of local principalities. But now the principalities have disappeared. Instead of the submissive poor, dependent on charity and political help, you have articulate people with a sense of entitlement. Very few have any reason for gratitude to ward boss; most probably have a feeling of contempt for politicians. And outside the urban areas, where these changes in dependency have taken place, there are others reasons for the ties of party to have disappeared. The American population has become so mobile that it has lost the roots, the sense of community, that used to underlie political allegiance in the lower East side and the rural south alike.

So today there is little if any party loyalty. If John Sears wants to leave the high life of a columnist and go back to professional politics, he will almost certainly have to do it the way he did until New Hampshire: by working for an individual candidate, not for a party. We are in the age of atomized politics, without structure, without process except what the press supplies—accidentally and inadequately.

I happen to believe that it is urgently important to find some way of revitalizing the political parties—of making them, again, the vehicle for the choice of candidates and, at the same time, for the forming of coalitions that can govern. That brings me to the second part of my subject.

So far I have been talking about electing the president, and what the press has to do with that. Now I turn to the question of governing. If we are disappointed in the ability of recent presidents to govern, then once again I think the press bears some of the responsibility.

And there is disappointment with the performance of presidents. Everyone can see that. The gulf between what we expect from the occupant of the White House and what he delivers is a leading subject these days for journalists and political scientists alike. The most recent examination of the problem is a book by a British journalist, Godfrey Hodgson, with the title *All Things to All Men: The False Promise of the Modern American Presidency*. Hodgson sums up his argument as follows: "The paradox of the presidency is simply stated, if hard to resolve. Never has any office had so much power as the President of the United States possesses. Never has so powerful a leader been so impotent to do what he wants to do, what he is pledged to do, what he is expected to do and what he knows he must do."

That idea, the frustration of presidential power, is not new. One of the first academic president-watchers, Professor Richard Neustadt of Harvard, had a wonderful quotation in his 1960 book on the subject. Harry Truman, just before he left the oval office in 1953, said of his successor, "He'll sit here, and he'll say, 'Do this! Do that' and nothing will happen. Poor Ike—it won't be a bit like the Army. He'll find it very frustrating."

Hodgson sees the problem as one of institutional failure. The president cannot get things accomplished, he argues, because the structure of the office has not been modernized to cope with today's demands on it. He blames Franklin Roosevelt of all people. The argument is that F.D.R. invented the modern presidency, one dominating our politics, but did not create the machinery to go with it. Instead he relied on the force of his own personality to move Congress and have a responsive bureaucracy and build a party coalition and use the press. He succeeded, but he left future presidents no levers to push. And today members of Congress are preoccupied with their own survival in single-issue politics, the bureaucracy has taken on an unresponsive life of its own, the party has collapsed, and even the press in its new guise—television—has not lived up to its promise as an instrument of presidential power. "The modern presidency has come to depend too much on the media," Hodgson says. "It is not clear that the media can save it."

That is Hodgson's diagnosis. The president cannot meet expectations, he says, because he does not have effective power to move the system. Well, with all respect—as they say in Britain when they are about to give the back of the hand to someone's carefully constructed argument—I disagree. I think Hodgson, in looking at the imbalance between promise and performance in the White House, has started at the wrong end. In my view the first reason for the existing disappointment lies not in delivering too little but in promising too much.

When I followed President Carter in the campaign for a few days, I noticed how often he was asked in those meetings he held with citizens what he would do for particular groups and interests: for the elderly, for students by way of loans, for parochial schools, for housing, for refugees, for the sick, for the unemployed, for cities, for farms, for the automobile industry. You will not be surprised when I tell you that I never once heard him answer: "I can do nothing," or, "I will do less." He told every group that he had its interests at heart and planned to do more for it.

When I was with Governor Reagan, he said at practically every stop that it was time "to get the government off the backs of the people." That drew applause every time, including the day when he made a bus trip through the rich farms of central

Illinois. I thought to myself that day that the audiences would react a little differently if they thought he really meant it—and would get the government out of the business of subsidizing farmers. But in fact he promised to do even better for farmers. And he endorsed the federal loan to Chrysler and the loan to New York City that he once said he prayed every night would never be granted.

As both Carter and Reagan talked about federal support for all those different activities, what struck me was that not so long ago—in my lifetime, at any rate—none of them would have been considered the responsibility of the president of the United States. He would not have been expected to provide loans to college students or assure sales of wheat or care for the sick or rescue failing automobile companies. The federal government would not have been expected to do those things—not before 1933, and in most cases not until long after World War II. In that regard we have gone through what amounts to a political revolution. The shifting of enormous responsibility to the center. Things that used to be the concern of state and local government, or of no government at all, are now considered to be the business of federal government. And in political terms that very largely means the president. He is our one visible national political figure, so the expectations run to him.

We have gone so far in expecting the president to solve our problems that I am reminded of the scene in Shakespeare's *Henry V,* the night before the battle of Agincourt, when the King wanders in disguise through his own camp. He hears from the ordinary soldiers how they fear death—and believe the King will bear responsibility for whatever happens to them. Then, alone, he says to himself:

> Upon the King! let us our lives, our souls,
> Our debts, our careful wives,
> Our children and our sins lay on the King!

Walter Mondale put it somewhat less elegantly. Speaking of the burdens of the White House, he said to a friend recently, "I told Carter one day, I said I got this figured out. We're the nation's fire hydrant."

How did it happen, this transformation of what not so long ago was a country of divided responsibilities, local and national, private and public, into a nation where everyone looks to the center—to the White House? To some extent it was the inevitable result of technological change, of the revolution in transportation that brings distant countries—and their weapons—next door, and in communications that connect us all together in an instant. When the president is right there on your television screen, talking to the Raffertys about their problems in Gloucester City, you naturally think of him as the person upon whom you can lay your debts, your sins, your soul. But the press has greatly helped the change.

The romance of the modern presidency owes a lot to the press. It is natural for journalists to write about good guys and bad guys, heroes and villains; in that, we are still in the straightforward days of nineteenth-century fiction. For much of the postwar period the press made a hero of the president, whoever he was. He was the noble, progressive figure, fighting a lonely battle against the narrow-minded, entrenched forces in Congress and among the special interest. That was true on the domestic side when Harry Truman struggled unsuccessfully for liberal legislation and later when John Kennedy pushed for the tax and civil rights bills that became law only after his death. It was even more true in foreign affairs, where an overwhelming press consensus formed around the interventionist, anti-Communist outlook of successive postwar administrations, regardless of party. How many now remember when Senator Robert Taft, that stalwart Republican, opposed the North Atlantic Treaty as involving the United States too deeply in the problems of Europe? Not many, I suspect, because the episode was blotted out by the development of the foreign policy consensus, cheered on by the press. And the president was at the center of it. He had superior knowledge, superior wisdom; he alone could deal with the hostile forces in the world, and Congress and the rest of us had better stop bothering him and let him get on with the job.

The press worship of the presidency came to an end during the Vietnam War. It was not possible to go on believing in the wisdom, not to mention the truthfulness, of political leaders who kept saying that the war was going well when the opposite was demonstrably the case. Even the newspapers closest to the establishment, those that had played the leading part in creating the myth of all-knowing presidential wisdom, began to take a more critical view. There was a watershed in the Pentagon Papers case, when the *New York Times* set out to publish excerpts from a secret official history of the Vietnam War—something the *New York Times* might not have done before disillusionment about presidential policy set in—and President Nixon tried to stop the publication. When that clash was over, and the courts had allowed the *Times* to go on publishing, a leading law review article on the case said it symbolized "the passing of an era in which newsmen could be counted upon to work within reasonably well-understood boundaries." It said "the *New York Times* by publishing the Papers, did not merely reveal a policy debate within the Executive Branch; it demonstrated that much of the press was no longer willing to be merely an occasionally critical associate devoted to common aims, but intended to become an adversary threatening to discredit not only political dogma but also the motives of the nation's leaders."

Then came Watergate, destroying what little remained of the symbiotic relationship between the press and the presidency. After Watergate a political scientist writing about the decline of presidential power, Samuel P. Huntington, said the press had in effect joined the opposition. That may be putting it a bit colorfully. But I think there can be no doubt that since Vietnam and Watergate the American press has taken a much more negative view of all holders of political power—more negative and more aggressive. Sometimes, reading the latest investigative takeout, one gets the sense that everything and everyone in official life is presumptively corrupt. We even had a book this year suggesting that the justices of the Supreme Court were knaves or fools. The evidence was thin or nonexistent, but editors eagerly serialized the book and readers read it. We want to know the worst about anyone in public life these days, and at least some in the press are ready to supply it.

Billy Carter testifying before the Senate Judiciary subcommittee investigating his dealings with Libya.

The president is the main target of this new presumption of official guilt. We all know examples. One is what came to be called Billygate. The very name is indicative of the tendency to presume guilt. The affair of Billy Carter and Libya had nothing in common with Watergate. There was no showing that President Carter had misused official power to help his brother, or condoned Billy's outrageous behavior. Senator Bob Dole, not exactly a loving admirer of Jimmy Carter said after his participation in the Senate investigation that there were "no parallels with Watergate." But Billygate it was called, and Billygate it no doubt remains in the minds of many citizens—with all that implies. It was the press that coined that name. It was the press that produced successive dramatic disclosures that, on reflection, meant nothing. One was the story—under page one headlines in the *New York Times* and the *Washington Post*—that Billy Carter had been shown "classified State Department cables" about his trip to Libya. Shocking, isn't it? But it should not have shocked serious journalists, because they know that 99 percent of what the government classifies is routine material, not really secret at all. Indeed, that was one of the main arguments made by the *Times* in the Pentagon Papers case, and it is part of the experience of every newspaper man and woman in Washington. Very few classified documents contain true state secrets, and the cables about Billy Carter's trip to Libya were not among those few. They turned out to be utterly innocuous, routine messages noting where Billy Carter had gone and what he had done. Those interested in a detailed discussion of the press's performance in Billygate should see the impressive piece by Robert M. Kaus in the October issue of the *Washington Monthly*.

In a conversation with reporters the day after the election President Carter said:

> In the post-Watergate era the press and the public are legitimately interested in personal fallibilities. The allegations that I cheated by borrowing money from Bert Lance's bank and in effect channeling money through my warehouse into my campaign fund in 1976 received headline treatment for weeks. . . . Those allegations were false, and they were finally announced to be completely false. But that series of charges, headlines, news stories about my cheating as a candidate in 1976 obviously made a small impression on the American consciousness. The same for allegations that Hamilton Jordan did something that was illegal in the use of drugs. That was ultimately shown to be made by three convicted felons who lied. But you know the impressions still exists. Rosalynn saw one of the Moral Majority preachers this morning say that Hamilton Jordan's use of drugs is something that the American electorate acted on last night by putting a true Christian in the White House. . . . Those kinds of things . . . are part of the American consciousness, and I'm sure they made an impression on some people.

Was the President wrong in thinking that those charges stuck to a degree, even though false?

The legacy of Watergate and Vietnam—the tendency to suspect the worst of public officials, even to presume bad motives—is intensified by the fact of competition in the press. No newspaper or magazine or network wants to be outdone by its competitor, so it tends to push the story a little harder than it might otherwise. I think we saw that factor at work in the effort to come up with new Chappaquiddick exposés when Senator Kennedy entered the race for the nomination last fall. The *New York Times* published a lengthy piece about some vanished records of Kennedy telephone calls after the accident. Its exact import was hard to understand, at least for me it was, but there was an intimation of something sinister. Blair Clark in the *Columbia Journalism Review* called the piece derivative, trivial, irrelevant, and tendentious. I think it was an example of a competitive urge to get a new angle on a story whose unvarnished substance raised legitimate doubts about a politician.

I am not against competition in journalism; I am for it. I am not against tough investigative stories; I am for them. But I think the competitive exigencies combine with a presumption of official guilt to produce an unrelentingly critical tone that makes life very difficult for government and its officials. How easy would any of us, reporters or editors, find it to do our work if everything we did or said was automatically suspect? I ask no tears of sympathy for politicians; as Mr. Truman said, "If you can't stand the heat, get out of the kitchen." The concern, rather is for us, the governed. For we are the victims if the tone of our politics goes beyond skepticism to the weakening of necessary authority especially the authority of the president.

In her gripping novel, *The King Must Die,* May Renault builds on Greek myth to describe the bloody political system in the island kingdom of Naxos. Every year the ruling king fought a stranger just arrived on the island—and died. The winner became king, for a year, and then lost his crown and life. Sometimes it seems as if America in the second half of the twentieth century is following the Naxos model and regularly destroying its king. No president has served two terms now for 20 years. There is a crisis of presidential authority.

Of course the press has not sought that result, or been principally responsible for it. The accident of fate that killed John F. Kennedy was largely responsible, in my judgment. And the presidents who followed him followed a course of deception and abuse of power that had destructive effects on the office. There was a reaction against the abuses of Lyndon Johnson and Richard Nixon, rightly so. Congress took steps to clamp down on presidents. It enacted an automatic special prosecutor law so stringent that a felon's unsupported charge against a White House assistant can lead to a damaging legal process. And Congress intruded deeply into what had been an area left largely to executive discretion, foreign policy. From an imperial presidency we have gone to a presidency that has to wheedle and cajole for any discretion at all. And the press, while not responsible for the events that started the deterioration of presidential authority, has intensified that trend, making life in the post-Vietnam, post-Watergate era difficult for any president.

One more factor should be mentioned. The press—again out of its inevitable nature, not out of any conspiratorial animosity—has tended more and more to penetrate the privacy of presidents. In fact presidents have invited that attention, thinking perhaps that homely details of their families and their mode of life would make them more popular. But the result has actually been to strip them of an element of mystery that many think is essential to effective leadership. Can you imagine President DeGaulle inviting the press in to look through his bedroom and clothes closet? Professor Henry Graff of Columbia was right, I think, when he wrote of today's American president:

> His life is under such relentless scrutiny that he can only seem ordinary, never extraordinary. No man is a hero to his valet and America is now a nation of valets. The framers of the Constitution did not intend—least of all expect—that the President would be constantly on view. But the Presidents of the last generation gave up the advantages of remoteness—not to say aloofness—which historically is the strength of leadership in great nations.

The press and the presidency need each other and affect each other and do each other good and harm. They are locked in deadly embrace.

The president relies on the press, especially television, as his last best hope of moving the system—his hope of effective power. But the public is less and less interested. Nearly half of it does not bother to vote. The public has turned off because of disappointed expectations—expectations aroused by the press in collaboration with the candidates. It has grown cynical in part because the press has shown it every wart on the president's face—and some that are not there.

We need a press that is skeptical of authority—better that than the often deferential collaboration of the postwar years. But the press should also recognize the need for some authority, and recognize that we are not overendowed with it in this country right now. We need what Judge Murray Gurfein said in the Pentagon Papers case: an obstinate press, cantankerous press, a ubiquitous press. But we also need a press that seeks deeper understanding. We need less scandal and more analysis, less personalization of the president and more appreciation that this continental country cannot be effectively managed in detail from the center by any single human being.

To put it a different way, I think we need more modesty on both sides: a press and presidents more aware of their limitations. That is not a ringing conclusion, but is a necessary one if we are to escape from the vicious political circle of frustrated expectations.

3

The Nightly News: A Leap of Faith versus the Bottom Line

March 10, 1982

Perspective

Television producer Fred W. Friendly was once known for giving aspiring young reporters a printed card with a quote from Ed Klauber, an early pioneer of broadcast news, that espoused his philosophy of news and the duty of journalists. It stated that news analysts "should bear in mind that in a democracy it is important that people not only should know but should understand, and it is the analyst's function to help the listener to understand, to weigh and to judge, but not to do

The Nightly News: A Leap of Faith versus the Bottom Line

the judging for him." As the speaker for the Third Annual Chet Huntley Memorial Lecture, Friendly deals with a topic that had, by 1982, been his driving concern for many years—the need for an hour-long news broadcast to give viewers a full, balanced picture of the day's news. Since broadcast news had become not only an accepted form of journalism, but in many cases the *only* media that many Americans turned to for their news, Friendly supported an increase in the time allotted to nightly news broadcasts on the major networks. As many journalists have argued in the past—Chet Huntley among them—half an hour just wasn't enough.

For many years, television news broadcasts struggled to be accepted by the public, and by print journalists, as a respectable form of news media. As NBC News executive Reuven Frank has noted in his 1991 book, *Out of Thin Air: The Brief and Wonderful Life of Network News,* many journalists—even those associated with television news in its early years—"thought news was what you read in the *New York Times,* and broadcasting's role was to discuss it and explain it." Through the professionalism of early pioneers in the field such as Edward R. Murrow, Chet Huntley, and David Brinkley, television news took on a journalistic character of its own, gaining the respect and appreciation of wide audiences.

Nevertheless, few anticipated that television would ever overtake printed media as *the* major source of information for the American public. Friendly cites statistics showing that, by the early 1980s, more than half of the American public received their daily dose of news solely from television.

Until the mid-1960s, nightly news lasted only 15 minutes. Expansion was inevitable as the medium grew more popular, but is 30 minutes, which is then cut back by almost a third due to commercial time, enough to report the news adequately? Friendly argues otherwise. Expansion to an hour-long broadcast, he notes, is much less about "the bottom line" than about the responsibility television news now bears to its viewing audience.

Now, more than 10 years after Friendly's lecture, television news broadcasts can receive top billing. For example, Diane

Sawyer's "Prime Time Live" is competitive in its 10 P.M. slot against the popular drama "L.A. Law," CBS's "60 Minutes" has won top ratings in its Sunday evening spot for many years, and news formats have virtually taken over early morning programming. Broadcasting mogul Ted Turner was so confident in the American public's interest in current affairs programming that he created Cable News Network (CNN) in 1980, an all-news station that has been embraced by television viewers across the world. Despite the fact that the success of television news has spawned a wealth of "tabloid TV" news programs, no one can deny that quality broadcast news accounts for a considerable share of the high ratings. The ranks of television news overflow with internationally recognized, widely respected journalists. As Friendly so aptly notes of this postindustrial age we live in, "What we don't know *could* kill us."

The Nightly News: A Leap of Faith versus the Bottom Line

Introduction of Fred W. Friendly
by Lester Crystal

Lester Crystal, a senior executive producer at NBC for almost 15 years, has also been a member of the selection committee for the Chet Huntley Memorial Lecture Series. A four-time recipient of the Emmy Award for his work with NBC, Crystal has been the executive producer of the highly acclaimed "MacNeil-Lehrer NewsHour" since 1983. He introduced the third lecturer in the Huntley series, former NBC News president Fred Friendly.

Introduction

I feel particularly privileged tonight to introduce our guest speaker, partly because I had the privilege and honor of knowing and working with Chet Huntley, and partly because of who our speaker is.

When Fred Friendly began preparing tonight's lecture, he called me and said, "I'm curious about something." And many of his colleagues will tell you that's something he's said hundreds of times. He said, "I'm curious about a reference to Walter Cronkite in Supreme Court Justice William O. Douglas's autobiography."

In the book, Douglas talks about the climate of fear during the peak of McCarthyism, and how most newsmen were intimidated by it. Three exceptions, Douglas said, were Elmer Davis, Edward R. Murrow, and Walter Cronkite. Douglas wrote that Cronkite was struggling at the time to keep alive as a commentator in Los Angeles, but he had trouble getting sponsors because he was considered to be too liberal. In his book, Douglas said a friend of his who manufactured mattresses and who cherished the liberal tradition kept Cronkite on the air by sponsoring and helping sponsor his programs.

Fred Friendly told me he thought Justice Douglas may have been wrong in his book, that the Los Angeles commentator was not Walter Cronkite. Well, we did some checking, and we found, as Fred suspected, that the West Coast broadcaster that Justice Douglas was writing about was, in fact, Chet Huntley.

We checked the files further and found that Chet not only refused to be intimidated at that time, but he struck back at those who were trying to intimidate him. When, in 1954, a woman accused him of being a Communist, Chet Huntley filed a $200,000 libel and slander suit against her. He won, out of court, with a settlement of $10,000 and a public apology from

The Nightly News: A Leap of Faith versus the Bottom Line

the woman that was published in the *Los Angeles Evening Herald and Express*.

So, it's particularly fitting that tonight's speaker is someone who also refused to be cowed by McCarthyism. Chet Huntley's gutsy reaction is buried in the files. Fred Friendly and Ed Murrow's stand against McCarthyism, with that historic "See It Now" program, is a famous and important part of our political history.

Fred's string of titles, which I'm sure most of you know of—producer and collaborator with Murrow on "See It Now" and "CBS Reports," president of CBS News, professor at Columbia School of Journalism, adviser to the Ford Foundation, author—more than qualify him to deliver the Chet Huntley Memorial Lecture.

But it is Fred Friendly's nature that distinguishes him as someone very special. Fred Friendly has a fire in his belly—a fire about the world around us, and about what broadcast journalists do. That is why "See It Now" and "CBS Reports" were so acclaimed. That is why he walked out of the CBS News presidency when his network refused to carry live the Senate hearings on Vietnam. That is why he is such an inspiring teacher.

Many students tell of an incident a couple of years ago, when he planned to show one of his classes a tape of the "60 Minutes" report on Colonel Herbert. As I'm told, there were elaborate preparations—the class was to start early, tape machines were provided—and at the start, Fred held up the cassette and asked a student to look at the label.

He said, "What does this suggest to you?" The student looked at the cassette and the label and said it suggested that it was a cassette of the "60 Minutes" interview with Colonel Herbert. Fred waved the cassette and said, "Wrong!" An incorrect cartridge had been put in the case. Then he thundered, "I want this engraved on your retinas—inanimate objects are out to screw you."

Fred has inspired us all—about the basic issues, and about our responsibilities. Shortly before his 65th birthday, he told an interviewer, "If I had a magic wand, and could have whatever I

Introduction

wanted as a birthday present, it would be an hour-long nightly news on all three networks." He didn't get his magic wand, but he hasn't given up hope. And he's going to talk to us tonight about his birthday wish.

Fred has worked on his presentation tonight in the way he tackled documentaries years ago. More than 50 interviews, I'm told, and many, many hours of preparation. It's more of a reporting job than a lecture. Well, he was a journalist first, and a teacher second. Tonight, we're going to hear from both.

Fred W. Friendly

Born in New York City, Fred W. Friendly has been a driving force behind radio and television journalism for more than fifty years. In the 1940s he produced the "I Can Hear It Now" record series with Edward R. Murrow and the "Hear It Now" CBS radio series with Walter Cronkite. In the 1950s Friendly and Murrow coproduced the groundbreaking "See It Now" program, which brought new respect to television journalism through its in-depth coverage of significant current affairs, such as its famous report on Senator Joseph McCarthy. Friendly went on to produce "CBS Presents" (later "CBS Reports"). Friendly became president of CBS News in 1964, but resigned only two years later over the network's refusal to provide live coverage of the Senate hearings on Vietnam. He was Edward R. Murrow Professor of Journalism at Columbia University (1968–75), and later Edward R. Murrow Professor Emeritus. He has been responsible for public television programs that gather scholars, officials, and journalists to discuss controversial issues confronting government and society. Friendly has also authored a number of books, including Due To Circumstances Beyond Our Control *(1967),* The Good Guys, the Bad Guys, the First Amendment *(1975), and, with Martha J. H. Elliot,* The Constitution: That Delicate Balance *(1984).*

The Nightly News: A Leap of Faith versus the Bottom Line

*L*ast spring I was invited to talk to the Neiman Fellows in Cambridge. In the course of my ramblings, I answered a question about the nightly news by stating that attempting to report the day's flood of national and international news in 22 1/2 minutes was obscene. I believed that, because every night 50 million people get up from their television sets reasonably satisfied that they've seen it all, that "that's the way it is." The following week, a network news executive addressed the same audience. When asked about the remark of the previous week's speaker, he replied, "There was a bit of sophistry in Mr. Friendly's reporting. The fact is, on some days there is not a lot of news for a national audience . . . given our definition of 'news.'"

When I read that exchange, the first thing I did was look up the definition of the word *sophistry:* "A subtle, tricky, superficially plausible but generally fallacious method of reasoning." Tricky I have been called before, a bit superficial perhaps, but never subtle. Next, I turned on my television set and watched two hours of local news followed by 30 minutes of network news. The contrasts were startling. I was bombarded by frenetic accounts of fires, muggings in subways, teenage prostitution, sports, weather, and actors and authors plugging their latest works. I wondered whether the casual viewer could separate the local news, with all its psychedelic trappings, from the national news broadcasts. I also thought anew about the dynamics and economics of an industry where the hyped trivia of violence and escapism were worth four times as much air time as serious news reports of the events of a nation

Fred W. Friendly

desperately attempting to straighten out its fiscal mess and a world trying not to extinguish itself. I wondered if the public was ever puzzled by this disparity in news coverage. How could it be that there was sufficient local and regional news to fill two hours (minus commercials) but not enough national and international news to fill 22 1/2 minutes? Was not the root of this apparent contradiction in the definition of that elusive word *news*? So when Les Crystal called me up in behalf of your committee to ask me to deliver the Chet Huntley Memorial Lecture, I did not have to be coaxed. I knew instantly what I would talk about—and that it would require more than 22 1/2 minutes.

As we meet tonight to honor Chet Huntley, television news has reached a fork in the road, and that "road not taken," to borrow from Robert Frost, could "make all the difference." Twenty years ago, NBC and CBS made the bold decision that 15 minutes of national and international news was not sufficient, and the half-hour evening news was born. That watershed decision was not traumatic. Yet in 1982, the proposal by all three networks to provide an hour of news is stalled in a heated confrontation between the local station owners and their networks.

The battle has all the tensions and misunderstanding of the arms race—two powerful forces arrayed against each other, distrust versus distrust, greed versus greed, inventory versus overkill, "Trojan horse" versus "the news as hostage," to use the rhetoric of the two ideological camps.

Few issues on the American agenda are more crucial than the prospect of expanding the nightly news in order to achieve new dimensions of comprehension through innovative forms of presentation that only a liberated time frame will make possible. The public has the biggest stake in this debate, which is too important to be left completely in the hands of the television industry.

I realize it is far easier for a mangy old lion from Morningside Heights to advocate the hour news than it is for network executives to make the decision or station managers to go along with it. The agony of this decision combines all the elements:

The Nightly News: A Leap of Faith versus the Bottom Line

news as profit center, as a basic staple of democracy, even the meaning of that evolving term *news*.

Every year at Columbia I begin one of my classes by forcing the students to define *news* and *newsworthy*. It may sound easy, but it's a damn tough assignment, and it has nothing to do with men biting dogs. For a long time, we've thought of "news" as events, happenings—plane crashes, embassy takeovers, election returns, yes, fires. But on a shrunken planet where information is relayed with the speed of light, we have to expand the definition beyond mere events. We constantly have to redefine news and our methods of relaying and explaining information to the public. No longer can we tell it as soon as we hear it, we have to tell it no sooner than we can understand it. *Flash* was the signal of Walter Winchell. *Think* was the summons of the journalist we honor tonight.

In April of 1970, Chet Huntley challenged us to redefine news: "News is no longer the bare bones of what happened . . . or where . . . or when . . . and neither is it a palatable and brief quote . . . of some V.I.P.," he wrote. "It is also what is somewhere in the minds of men," and he implored, "we must get it on the air."

Fifty years earlier, long before there was such an instrument as television or even radio news, Walter Lippmann saw the need for a continuing expedition "to bring to light the hidden facts, to set them into relationship with each other and make a picture of reality on which citizens can act."

In 1982, television may be the most powerful, most pervasive medium, but it does not yet do an adequate job of providing a reliable picture of the world. Television journalism is at its best during the crisis—live reporting of a plane crash, an assassination, or a presidential resignation. The networks also demonstrate their abilities during historic events—a space shuttle liftoff, an election, or a papal visit. But television falters when it comes to explaining such thorny issues as nuclear disarmament, human rights, or supercorporate mergers and their impact on productivity, or why Ruth Friendly buys a Honda instead of a Ford. And in this day and age, what we don't know *could* kill us.

This inability to cover complex issues is particularly frightening when we look at the way most people get their news. In the late 1950s, a Roper survey reported that 51 percent of the public got most of its information from television; by the 1980s it had risen to 64 percent. Almost half of those people rely on television as the sole source of news. Those statistics may not represent the highly educated or the heavy-dose news consumers, but they probably reflect a profile of the population. Informed or not, each citizen's vote counts the same. Public opinion forsaken is as damaging a defect as public health ignored. Apathy is becoming a disease of democracy, and a democratic form of government cannot function with an ignorant or indifferent electorate seized with what Lippmann called "violent prejudice, apathy, preference for the curious trivial against the dull important and the hunger for the sideshows and three-legged calves." I've never seen a three-legged calf on television, but last January I did watch a Labrador retriever who had reputedly predicted the winners of the last two Superbowls.

There are many reasons for television's shortcomings. The temptation to go for the exciting or bizarre picture rather than the substance is one. Enormous costs of newsgathering and production under breakneck pressure is another. But the primary roadblock to excellence is that television has that 22 1/2 minute handicap.

Walter Cronkite once asked, "Can we honestly expect to illuminate our nation's and the world's darkest corners each day in that little segment, that sliver of time?" Cronkite voiced concern that if we try to shoehorn "ten kilos of material into our one-kilo sack" we will distort what we do communicate. "Overcompression of gas creates a great deal of heat—sometimes to an explosive degree," he said. "With an hour, we could expand each item just enough to add one explanatory phrase that might increase understandability and obviate misunderstanding."

Most television journalists would agree, but not all. David Brinkley, when asked about the case for an hour of network news, responded with the economy of language that is almost

The Nightly News: A Leap of Faith versus the Bottom Line

his trademark: "If I had to do an hour tomorrow, I wouldn't quite know what to do with it. . . . If a story is covered adequately by television standards in two minutes, I'm not sure it'd be improved by running it four minutes."

I differ. In 22 1/2 minutes, all you can do is an index, at best a digest. To be sure, it's superior to the flashing-light bulletins from Times Square or the junk news from too many newspapers, radio and television stations, but it is a faint shadow of what the network news divisions are capable of. ABC's "Nightline," "Sunday Morning," the "MacNeil-Lehrer NewsHour," "60 Minutes," and often the "Today Show" are examples of what can be accomplished by dedicated journalists when there is sufficient air time and especially when the assignment is examining one or two significant stories in depth rather than "hopscotching the world for headliners," as the Camel News Caravan of early television used to call its capsulated news.

Today, all three networks possess the caliber of journalistic skills necessary to produce the levels of multidimensional reporting that distinguish our better newspapers. But the nightly news hole is already crowded to overflow. Last month the *Los Angeles Times* ran a long front-page profile of Justin Dart, the California millionaire who claims to be President Reagan's "kingmaker" and confidante. It's a magnificent piece with lots of insights on how this administration works. A fortnight ago, the *Washington Post* published the comprehensive report on the sad plight of the *New York Daily News*. This Monday, on page two of the *New York Times,* there was a brilliant essay by Joseph Lelyveld on "The Life and Death of a Nonconformist Afrikaner" minister and his black parish. Broadcast journalists are denied such extended "enterprisers," as they are called, because they may seem too long to viewers who have grown accustomed to the staccato pace of television. Bill Moyers calls it "speed-reading journalism." The chief deterrent is not talent or energy, but always the clock.

Twenty-two and a half minutes means every night there are stories that don't get on the air, because there just isn't enough time. The process of deciding what goes on the news becomes a daily auction—sometimes the winner being the most significant stories, but often the truly important is sacrificed for the sensational or urgent. Whoever heard of El Salvador until it was on fire? When did we start seeing in-depth reports from Iran, or Poland, or Detroit, and when will the nightly news provide more than a glancing reference to Guatemala?

Twenty-two and a half minutes also means that most reports are reduced to two or three minutes and some to 30 or 40 seconds and even less. The high priority to get as much on as possible often means truncating a Supreme Court decision into an almost incomprehensible 20-second blurb. Thoughtful pieces are hacked away at until they have pace and a sense of alarm that may be good for the ratings, but that process can mutate that which was meant to illuminate into a distortion. No journalist sets out to do that; imperceptibly it gets out of hand when the "yet but" school of reporting and analysis is crowded out by the inexorable force of the stopwatch. It is always difficult to prove or evaluate the levels of distortion caused by compression. A former student of mine who is now a correspondent for a television network, shared with me a sensitive, brief analysis of his own indoctrination to capsulated news. He wrote:

> Any story can be done in a minute-forty-five . . . but if you are dealing with a story that involves a complicated issue, or a story that has more than two sides, you are in serious trouble. . . . There is only time for black and white. . . . The problem is, our world is mostly shades of gray.
>
> At 1:45 things have to be presented in terms that people can easily grasp. Unfortunately, that often leads to oversimplification and a reliance on stereotypes. . . . If a story on a troubled nuclear plant runs 1:45 instead of 1:52, you may lose the provocative quote from a power company official who says that "the worst possible nuclear accident is not a classic line breakdown like we had at Three Mile Island, but a war over Middle East oil." . . . You're left instead with something like "utility officials insist the plant is safe." Not exactly the same thing. But it saves four seconds. The only remedy is expansion of air time.

Some other recent examples of compression at the expense of clarity, and perhaps fairness:

The Nightly News: A Leap of Faith versus the Bottom Line

February 17. David Stockman spent five hours up on the Hill. When I watched the nightly news, I was struck by how little I heard from Stockman. What a revealing five- to eight-minute piece that testimony and the congressional hard questioning would have made. I'm sure that, with an hour newscast, one or more of the networks would have done it. Then the viewer would have had a much clearer idea of what went on at the hearing. What bothered me most about the coverage was the virtually unchallenged platform the networks unwittingly provided Stockman's critics.

February 18. At his press conference, President Reagan made some more errors and challenged the press, waving his undisclosed list of answers to previous allegations of error. But that night, on television, no one discussed the significance—or lack of significance—of these errors. No one discussed the press/presidential relationship—both possible in an hour's news. (Over the weekend, NBC *did* examine some of President Reagan's perceptions of how we became involved in Vietnam. But that only illustrated the potential of the evening news—given enough air time.)

March 2. The Senate of the United States passed the antibusing bill by a margin of 20 votes. It was the lead story for most newspapers, and it was the most significant victory to date for those conservatives who advocate legislation that could strip the federal courts of their jurisdiction over such conflicts as busing, school prayer, and abortion. CBS News reported that important story in 20 seconds, ABC in 30 seconds, and NBC in 90 seconds. Poor news judgment? Probably. But the time bind of 22 1/2 minutes makes it almost impossible to provide the kind of analysis this historic bill deserves as it moves to the House of Representatives.

Often television tries to tell a story when it really doesn't have time to tell it completely, and therefore only tells part of the picture, leaving people with the impression they have the full story. Actually, they have been benignly deceived; they have been shortchanged without knowing it. The tragedy is that many viewers believe they are getting all the news, so they don't bother reading a newspaper.

If this were a documentary instead of a lecture, I would now run for you two brief excerpts from recent broadcasts.

First, I would run a tape of a brief commentary by Jeff Greenfield, which I saw on the "CBS Morning News" of February 9th. He asks, "What is news? What stories deserve to get on network newscasts?" Greenfield illustrates how all three networks had, on a given night, run as much or more material on the von Bullow trial as they had on El Salvador. He sums up his piece as follows:

> The two key questions, I think, are these. First, for years, TV news has been trying to get cameras into courtrooms, a fight which now is being won in more and more states. The argument has always been the public's right to know. The reality seems to be that TV wants to do exactly what the print press has been doing for decades. It wants to show you the juiciest, most sensational of cases for the enjoyment of the audience. And what better than a case which has sex, money, social status, and a charge of attempted murder—a sort of real-life *Dallas*.
>
> Second, network news organizations say they must have more time, that a half hour a night—22 minutes—isn't enough to cover stories of critical importance, such as a war in El Salvador, which could affect American interests and perhaps lives. But if time is really that precious, then why is a trial of no imaginable long-lasting significance worth so much of this terribly scarce and valuable time?

Jeff Greenfield is right on target. The need for expanding the news is not going to be demonstrated by frittering away any valuable time in pursuit of fleeting ratings. If the concept of an expanded news has no vision other than more of the same or an extended electronic tabloid, then the local stations's claim that they can do it just as well will remain unchallenged.

Tape two in our documentary is priceless and provocative. It goes to the heart of the argument by local stations managers that they and not the networks should be providing expanded news.

The Nightly News: A Leap of Faith versus the Bottom Line

In the best journalistic tradition of bringing in-depth coverage of substantive issues to the public, Walter Cronkite moderated the Great Nuclear Arms debate in 1983. The participants were Henry Kissinger (top left); Michael Haseltine (bottom left), British defense minister; Paul Warnke (top right), former chief U.S. arms negotiator; and Igor Bahr (bottom right), German opposition leader.

Dave Marash, one of the most thoughtful journalists on New York local television, is conducting an extended interview with Walter Cronkite. It is part of a campaign to heighten viewer interest in WCBS-TV's local news, which had that week expanded from one hour to two. Marash asks Cronkite to comment on Charles Kuralt's recent speech in which he warned that the threat to the news media was not so much from the foes of a free press, but from "a new breed of manager who feels a greater responsibility to the bottom line than the public good."

Marash asks Cronkite if he was concerned about these trends. Cronkite agrees, "I can see . . . the trend. I don't think it has developed yet. I hope it's nipped in the bud. . . . They'll make a serious mistake if they try to alter the product to skirt what they think is the public taste." Marash drops his voice and with visible deference intones, "Amen, Walter." Coanchor Rolland Smith also thanks their visitor and then turns to the camera and announces, "Coming up next . . . in just a moment, some more news for you, and a live report on punk bowling, the latest fad."

Local news ranges from awful to not so awful, with some notable exceptions: WBBM-TV in Chicago, WCCO-TV in Minneapolis, WBZ-TV and WCVB-TV in Boston, KING-TV in Seattle, and WTVJ and WPLG in Miami, to name a few. As for those other happy newsrooms, it's not the teased hair and pearly-white smiles that I object to; it's all that giggling and fluff and gimmickry, which means a lot less responsible reporting. Punk bowling! Punk news!

My colleagues at the network news would protest that that kind of reporting couldn't happen here, but a few nights after the "punk bowling" report, I watched a three-minute network report from California on a training school for game show contestants. And it happened to be a very busy news day.

It is not being advocated here that all news has to be somber or that television has to be turned into a 19-inch wailing wall. What Andrew Rooney and Edwin Newman have proven is that humor and substantive journalism are quite compatible.

Television, as has been said, makes so much money doing its worst that it cannot afford to do its best . . . except in marginal time. We as a nation can't afford that price. It is not sophistry to state that this nation is edging close to a state of national emergency. Those citizens who wish to give the president time to save America under his electoral mandate are no less frustrated that those who are concerned that we are witnessing the gutting of America. How we defend ourselves, militarily, without taking so much from the poor that they despair may not be an emergency as dramatic as Pearl Harbor of even the Teheran embassy takeover, but it is there. The plight of our schools and universities and our commitment to the elderly may not be the "right stuff" compared to tense heroic on-camera liftoffs, but they are symptoms of a decaying orbit for the American dream.

So if the need is so imperative, why don't the networks utilize the gifted and often brilliant correspondents, producers, and editors of the news divisions? Why don't they proceed with an expanded, broadened, more insightful nightly news program? What's the hang-up?

It's the affiliated stations versus the network, and the tension is bitter. They all say it isn't money, but as one network president put it, "When they say it's not really the money, it's the money." The crux of the issue is whether the networks will make more and whether the stations will lose any.

To understand what's at stake, you have to understand the financial relationship between networks and their affiliated stations. Twenty years ago, television stations received 30 percent—and up to 40 percent—of their revenues in the form of compensation from network sales. Today, the compensation from the networks to the stations averages six to eight percent. Part of the reason for that low percentage is that the rate the station receives is arbitrary and ancient. There is an enormous gap between what the network receives from advertiters and what it passes on to the stations.

However, the stations make as much as 46 percent of their gross revenues from selling network adjacencies, the slots between programs and spots provided for them within network programs. In all, these can amount to as many as 500 to 600 commercials a week and are sold directly by the stations that are able to keep 100 percent of those sales (minus agency commissions). That means many millions of dollars. So while the network compensation has remained static, the number of spots and adjacencies—and the real money—has grown, sometimes at the expense of local programming. Of course, stations also earn money from their own programming, often more than 45 percent of their total revenues. In general, about five and a half hours originate locally. This is also a high-project area because the station has control over cost, and it can retain all the advertising revenue.

What's implicit in the expansion of the hour news is network encroachment on station time. The second half hour would come at a time when the station would otherwise be scheduling its own programs and generating its own revenues. The network plans vary. However, in general they propose a 6 to 7 P.M. EST feed with an update at 6:30 and, if required, at 7 P.M.

What kind of money are we talking about? The hour news broadcast would have approximately 24 thirty-second spots. Six to ten of these commercials would be sold by the local stations. Again, the numbers vary with each network. In addition, there would be more commercial time given to the stations at the middle break and at the end of the broadcast. Just to give you an idea, a 30-second spot in the network news sells for 35 to 50 thousand dollars. In New York, commercials in the local evening news sell for as much as $2,200. In Charlotte, North Carolina, it's $1,200 and in Boise, Idaho, it's $750. It's difficult to be precise about rates in an industry where there is no real rate card. It's a kind of floating auction, whatever the traffic will bear at any given time.

All three networks have at one time or another suggested that they expand the nightly news to an hour, offering all sorts of commercial tradeoffs. Each time it has come up, there has been sufficient uproar by the stations to put the plan on hold. The affiliates claim that they need every minute of their few local hours for local news and public service programs. The stations charge that the networks are greedy, that they simply want to sell more time at the expense of the local stations. They fear that the "glut" of available network spot sales would seriously cut into their ability to sell locally and regionally. Many stations managers believe that what is now a seller's market could quickly erode into a buyer's market, and profits might go down. Even though the networks have offered three to five minutes of lucrative commercials, the affiliates fear that a Trojan horse has been wheeled into their studios. Once they give up the half hour, they are concerned that the network will take back some of that time at contract renewal, invoking the high cost of production as rationale.

The Nightly News: A Leap of Faith versus the Bottom Line

To be fair, there are many station executives who favor the expanded evening news. Among them are Ancil Payne of KING Broadcasting with stations in the Northwest and Tom Chauncey of KOOL/Phoenix, whose stations helped pioneer the 30-minute news in 1962, and of course the managers of the network owned and operated stations. However, their affirmative views are dismissed by the present-day affiliate leaders as "relics of the past." The hard truth is that a survey in *Television/Radio Age* indicates that 57 percent of the affiliates oppose the hour news concept, although 45 percent would carry it if they were compensated in some way for the lost revenue. The GO/NO GO sign is always the dollar sign.

Not surprisingly, the networks accuse the stations of greed. Waving the sacred banner of news, they claim they are being held hostage by money-grubbing affiliates. As one network executive quipped, "We're going to allow them to sell three minutes in the expanded news. What do they want, all of it?"

Network executives point out that once the local stations learned that there was money to be made in high-gloss, low-substance local news, where they could insert as many as 16 minutes of commercials in an hour, they went all out expanding their local programs from 15 minutes to at least a half hour and even one, two or more hours in some markets.

One would think that the affiliated stations would want the Federal Communications Commission (FCC) to stay out of this family quarrel. After all, broadcasting has traditionally abhorred government regulation. Paradoxically, this time, many stations have wrapped themselves in the mantle of an FCC regulation called the Prime Time Access Rule (PTAR). In 1975, in a well-intentioned effort to counter the dominance of network programming over individual stations, the FCC enacted the PTAR. The regulation applies to the top 50 markets and mandates that local stations program at least one hour of prime time exclusive of the networks. However, the FCC did exempt one half hour of nightly news from this requirement. The concept was to encourage the stations to develop creative programs of their own. Although there have been some genuine achievements in this area, such as "P.M. Magazine," the "Muppets," and "Louisville Tonight," the regulation has stimulated a plethora of quiz and game shows, such as "Family Feud" and "Hollywood Squares." Only half of the network affiliate stations use this valuable time for the local public affairs that the Prime Time Access Rule was intended to free up. The networks view PTAR as an encroachment on the First Amendment, and CBS and NBC have petitioned the FCC to exempt an hour news program from the requirement. The stations are fighting that. PTAR is significant because it gives some stations a regulatory excuse for saying no to the the hourly news.

Another obstacle and point of obfuscation that needs to be dealt with is the time slot during which the hour news is transmitted. Group W (Westinghouse) insists that they could carry the hour news as long as it did not encroach on their local time. They suggest 10 to 11 P.M. EST. The networks consider this a smokescreen and doubt that Westinghouse stations or any other would want to run an hour of news just prior to the valuable 11 P.M. local news. The networks are convinced that William Baker, president of Westinghouse, favors the later slot because Westinghouse syndicates its successful program "P.M. Magazine" during the Prime Time Access period. The networks in turn resist scheduling the hour news in prime time because commercials in the news would produce less revenue. Thirty-second announcements in entertainment programs sell for an average of $75,000 and sometimes run as high at $160,000 for programs such as "Dallas" and "60 Minutes."

Joel Chaseman, who manages the four Post-Newsweek stations, recommends the 7:30 to 8:30 P.M. period. This concept is worth serious consideration. The failure and rapid turnover of new entertainment shows have reached ridiculous and extravagant expense—$800,000 and more for a single hour. An hour news, even with slightly lower ratings at the beginning, might turn out to be a more economical use of the time—in the long haul. The rate of return for "60 Minutes" wasn't very high at the beginning. Network programming generally has high casualty rates, but if they are going to fail, let them fail doing their best, not their worst.

The Nightly News: A Leap of Faith versus the Bottom Line

If the networks genuinely want the hour news, they are going to have to quiet the stations's fear that the Trojan horse—the encroachment of their time—will be their undoing. The networks will have to come up with a formula that will satisfy the financial needs of the affiliates, and that formula will have to stick. Since contracts between networks and affiliates can be in force for only two years, the stations and affiliates should ask the FCC to waive this rule so that the limit on the recapture of commercial spots in news can be sealed. Let the networks level with the stations about the projected costs of the expanded news and the actual incremental costs after the first two years. The stations suspect that the price tag of $25 million for additional newsgathering, long lines, and satellites is unrealistic; so do the newspersons, but for different reasons. There should be a precise accounting of what revenues the network produces in national sales, what the stations sell locally on the national spot market, and what the incremental costs of the expanded news will be so that, as they say in the trade, "both sides are made whole."

On the other hand, the networks must avoid adding so many commercials in order to satisfy their affiliates and to cover costs that the hour news becomes so cluttered as to be unwatchable. Bertrand Russell once said, "You have to be careful—sometimes they turn on the bath water so slowly, you don't know when to scream."

One other word of caution. If the networks expand to an hour of news, they must really make that commitment. There has been discussion of splitting the program into two half-hour segments and allowing the stations to take either the half hour or the hour. That would be a disaster. First, the stations who don't carry the second half would be embarrassed by the promos in the first half telling people to "stay tuned for more." Secondly, a first half hour that looks like the current one and a second that resembles "MacNeil-Lehrer" or "Nightline" or "60 Minutes" would not only lack identity, but would be needless duplication. The broadcast would be uneven. Some viewers would see an abbreviated version of the day's most important subject, others might see 30 minutes. It just wouldn't work.

If there is anything I would want you to take home with you, it's this: The hour news demands a leap of faith. The additional half hour must enlarge the public's understanding *geometrically,* not just arithmetically. It cannot simply mean 22 1/2 more minutes of two- and three-minute stories. It must be a dramatic step forward in television reporting, a coming of age of broadcast journalism.

I cannot describe what an hour news should look like any more than I could have predicted how "See It Now" would develop from its first small step of a live showing of the Atlantic and Pacific side by side in 1951. The journalists who proposed expanding those early 15-minute newscasts could not have given a slide presentation or produced a mock-up that illustrated that the half-hour news would eventually evolve into a "Huntley-Brinkley" or a "CBS Evening News."

This is an age of electronic wizardry, an age when communication skills have grown more complex and dazzling than any person as ancient as I could have ever imagined. In 1951, it took us two days to get a carton of 35-mm film from Pork Chop Hill in Korea to a cutting room in Manhattan, another four hours to develop and print it, and still more hours to edit it and get it on the air. During Vietnam, the improvement in 16-mm film and the advent of the jet narrowed the lag by a day. Today, videotape, ENG cameras and satellites mean that events in Iran, Poland, or El Salvador can be minutes, even seconds away. It doesn't make any sense to maintain today's staffs all over America and throughout the world and reduce the reporting to postage-stamp journalism.

National and international news is the birthright of the networks, but that news is being presented in a format that long ago lost its vitality . . . and has, by now, calcified. Producers have picked up its pace and added fancy graphics and the latest in electronic gimmickry . . . made it go so fast and look so slick that the viewer can barely tell what's missing. But the producers can't obscure the fact that they are working in a 20-year-old straitjacket.

Its constraints are best suited to handing what is one dimensional and easily understood, commodities hard to come by these days. Under its pressures, even the best journalists have trouble keeping track of the line between compression and oversimplification. The straitjacket may serve the purpose of accountants and managers seeking short-term profits, but so did the Friday night fights.

Much of U.S. industry is an emergency ward for once-flourishing enterprises so preoccupied with the short-term bottom line that they forgot to look at the horizon. For the automobile and steel giants, that may have been a deadly error. Henry Ford II once told me, "We saw all the signals for small cars. We just couldn't seem to change quickly enough."

The competition is no less fierce in the broadcasting business. Cable is buying up more and more of the sports events that used to be available to the networks. Can the day be far off when they can successfully compete with the networks's news services . . . and the revenues that go with them? Network news will survive only if it grows and provides a comprehensive service available to the public only from over-the-air television stations.

Broadcasting is a lucrative business far beyond the wildest dreams of those early settlers in the new electronic territory who wanted only a ticket (an FCC license) and a line (network affiliation). The profits from television have been enormous. "It's like owning the toll stations on a superhighway," one group owner told me. Broadcasting remains a worthy endeavor, and some local stations render a considerable public service with their news and public affairs. But the glue, the cement that holds the industry together is network news—whether it was radio during the Battle of Britain and Normandy or television during the four dark days after the Kennedy assassination or the civil rights struggles or the promises and threats of space technology in a thermonuclear age.

Television is here to stay, but whether over-the-air broadcasting can stand the competition of cable and satellites and even video games will depend upon whether broadcasters recognize the service that the news provides, and improve that service to meet the challenges and threats to our society.

Fred W. Friendly

By the time of the Persian Gulf War in 1990, cable television provided twenty-four hour a day news coverage.

Although the news chiefs of the networks advocate the hour news, their trumpet appears muted compared to the crusading voices one usually hears from the networks about such issues as the Equal Time Rule or the attempts by the Moral Majority to place limits on sex and violence. One also does not yet hear the vigorous voices of the chairmen of the boards vowing maximum efforts at every level to achieve the necessary expansion. It is my impression that those station managers who resist the hour news currently demonstrate more conviction than the network executives who champion it. The momentum seems to be running with the bottom line.

Ancil Payne of KING Broadcasting in Seattle is disturbed by the bottom-line fixation of his fellow affiliates: "Of course I

The Nightly News: A Leap of Faith versus the Bottom Line

care about the bottom line. But there can't be a bottom line on every program we do, on every minute of our schedule," he says. "Some programs such as the new, improved hour news we have to carry because it's right and because we owe it to the American people."

That's the ultimate bottom line of this warning. It was also Chet Huntley's vision. In 1967, he and his colleagues at NBC News were trying to break the 30-minute barrier. He said, "We have a gut feeling that if they give us a late-evening time slot [he meant 10 or 10:30], we can come up with higher ratings than some of the entertainment shows." Early evening or mid-evening—that vision of Chet Huntley is far more imperative today than it was 14 years ago. As Chet said, "We must get it on the air."

When Chet said that, an hour news would have been a giant step forward for any network. In 1982, standing still will be a giant and perhaps fatal step backward for network news.

4

Private Wars: The Government and Press Censorship

November 10, 1983

Perspective

What is the role of the free press in times of war? Should reporters be managed—told where to go and what to report so that the military's strategic position will not be compromised and the nation's support will not be challenged? Or should reporters be allowed free access to the conflict in order to exercise the maximum latitude in determining what the home public needs to know to be properly informed. In his speech discussing press coverage of the United States invasion of Grenada in October 1983, television news commentator John Chancellor argues that a substantial majority of Americans believed that the government was justified in denying the press the right to cover the invasion directly. Most journalists, however, do not agree with this assessment. According to them, the issue is one of censorship.

On October 25, 1983, President Ronald Reagan ordered an early morning invasion of Grenada, a small Caribbean island off the coast of Venezuela. The invasion was spurred by a seizure of power, earlier the same month, by a group that Reagan referred to as "a brutal gang of leftist thugs." The group had executed Grenadian Prime Minister Maurice Bishop as well as other members of the Cabinet, had shut down international airports on the island, and had imposed a "shoot on sight" curfew.

Particularly worrisome, according to U.S. government officials, was the presence on the island of some 1,000 American citizens, many of whom were students at St. George's University School of Medicine there. The Reagan administration also believed that Grenada's socialist government, with political ties to Cuba and the Soviet Union, represented a threat to the United States. One socialist government, headed by Maurice Bishop, had gained power in 1979 and was succeeded in October 1983 by a more radical one, which was headed by Deputy Prime Minister Bernard Coard.

Few Western reporters had been present on the island prior to the invasion; most had been removed at the time of Bishop's ouster. American journalists, denied access to the island during the invasion, were forced to rely for their information on U.S. government accounts of the fighting, telephone conversations with residents of the island, and radio reports from Grenada. Although a number of journalists were sent to the nearby island of Barbados, 150 miles northeast of Grenada, it was not until two days after the invasion began that a small contingent of press representatives was allowed to visit the scene of the fighting for a few hours, all under the close supervision of the U.S. armed forces. Gradually, over the next several days, additional reporters were allowed to visit Grenada.

Perspective

The offices of the Grenada People's Revolutionary Army at Ft. Rupert in St. George's after the U.S. invasion.

Chancellor argues that the Reagan Administration's refusal to allow the press access to the island in the initial stages of the invasion represented a significant violation of the American public's right to information. Perhaps the administration was

99

Private Wars: The Government and Press Censorship

reacting to the lesson of the Vietnam War, during which press access to the battleground is strongly believed to have contributed to the diminishing popularity of the war. But it is wrong, Chancellor points out, to assume that the presence of the press will necessarily turn the public against such an effort. The Grenada incident, which received much support from the American people, may have been even more popular if the press had been allowed to record it from the start.

As Chancellor states, wars and invasions in an era of hyper-technology are major media events. Censorship becomes more difficult when images can travel by satellite, in less than a second, from any part of the world to another. But on a small island like Grenada, roughly the size of Martha's Vineyard, it is relatively easy to keep the press at bay. Chancellor calls the Grenada invasion "a bureaucrat's dream: do anything, no one is watching."

Ultimately, what Chancellor finds most distressing is the reaction of the American people. In addition to supporting the war, the public generally expressed approval of the government's restrictions on press access. However, as Chancellor argues, the public was largely unaware of the censorship of the press in the incident. His lecture is a tribute to serious journalists, such as Chet Huntley, who opposed any obstructions to a balanced view of the news—even if that obstruction was the U.S. government.

Despite the uproar over press restrictions during the Grenada incident, it is not entirely clear whether reporters have received greater access in subsequent conflicts. During the Persian Gulf War, the American public may have felt that they were getting "the whole story," but were they? Journalists were on hand throughout the conflict, but their access to the troops and to the battlefields was limited. News organizations were dependent on briefing sessions run by the military, rather than being allowed to gather information for themselves. As *New York Newsday* columnist Sydney Schanberg has said of such government censorship, "the purpose . . . is to control and manipulate information, to sanitize and clean it up so that the war will sound more like a choir boy's picnic than the grungy thing that it is." As Chancellor notes, military conflicts tend to be much less popular when they are seen by the public without government censorship.

The reason is clear. If the government is the only source of information during wartime, the people are bound to see a distorted picture of the conflict, as the government will almost invariably present the most favorable version of the events. John Chancellor asks the American public to open its eyes to a serious problem, one that threatens the very foundation of our democratic system. As he puts it, "When your friendly government press agent . . . is your only source of information, you have to be worried."

Private Wars: The Government and Press Censorship

Introduction of John Chancellor by Elizabeth Drew

> *A writer and editor for such respected journals as the* Congressional Quarterly, Atlantic Monthly, *and the* New Yorker, *Elizabeth Drew has also been a regular panelist on "Meet the Press" (since 1988), and a commentator on "Inside Washington" (1973–92) and "Agronsky and Company" (1973-). She is the author of numerous books on political subjects, and the recipient of countless awards for her wide-ranging work. She introduced this year's Chet Huntley Memorial lecturer, television news commentator John Chancellor.*

Introduction

I happily accepted the invitation to introduce John Chancellor tonight, for two reasons. One is, I've been a colleague of John's for many years, as well as a neighbor of John and Barbara Chancellor's in Washington. The other reason is that I can introduce John from the heart. For, I feel that my dual exposure to John—personal and professional—does give me an insight into why he is a great journalist.

John began as a reporter for the *Chicago Sun-Times,* he joined NBC Television in Chicago, and along the way he's done just about everything. He's been a political correspondent, a foreign correspondent, the chief of the Moscow bureau, the host of the "Today Show," White House correspondent, and, of course, anchorman for "NBC Nightly News," and now the commentator on that program. Somewhere along the way he found time to be the director of the Voice of America.

But to me, the important thing is what sets him apart. To my mind, he has the two requirements of a great journalist: a zest for knowing and understanding what is going on, and character.

On the first point, John Chancellor just loves the news. He has an endless curiosity about it and enthusiasm for it. He wants not just to repeat it, but to really get at it, to really know what it's about before he tells us. And he never grows weary and jaded, which is, I assure you, a great occupational hazard.

Butt, no matter how much one knows about what's going on, you can't really convey it without character. By character, I mean integrity, honesty, and humanity—the simple virtue of being a good person.

It's that set of traits that set the great journalists apart from the merely good, aggressive, and clever. It's that set of traits that enables one to truly understand the events, and, most important, the people that one is dealing with. It is the ability to understand what is happening, and to have taste that enables one to win and hold, as John has, the public trust, and the respect and affection of his colleagues.

John Chancellor

Born July 14, 1927, in Chicago, Illinois, Chancellor attended the University of Illinois and began his career as a reporter for the Chicago Sun-Times. *He joined NBC News in 1950 as a radio newswriter for its Chicago affiliate (WMAQ), and later served as a foreign correspondent in Vienna, London, Moscow, and Brussels. He has covered such events as the Kruschev/Kennedy meeting in 1961 and President Gerald Ford's visits to East Asia and the Soviet Union. He also interviewed such dignitaries as Soviet Premiere Leonid Brezhnev, Israeli Prime Minister Yitzhak Rabin, and Egyptian President Anwar Sadat. In addition to his assignments as chief White House correspondent and host of the "Today Show," Chancellor has served as anchor for the "NBC Nightly News" (1970–81), and, since 1982, as commentator for NBC News. During his only time away from NBC News, Chancellor served (1965–67) as the director of the Voice of America; an appointment made by President Lyndon Johnson. Among his professional honors are the Distinguished Communications Medal and the Sol Taishoff award for excellence in broadcasting. In 1990 Chancellor authored* Peril and Promise: A Commentary on America, *in which he wrote a noteworthy analysis of the United States today.*

Private Wars: The Government and Press Censorship

I think if Chet Huntley had been here tonight, he would have wanted to talk about the press and the invasion of Grenada. One of the reasons we gather each year to memorialize Chet is that he understood what press freedom was all about, and fought for it whenever he could. He would be as upset as the rest of us by the exclusion of the press from the fighting in Grenada. His partner of many years, David Brinkley, testified against those press restrictions in Washington this week and so did I.

Let me say that this talk is not about the substance of the Grenadian operation. Reasonable people can argue about that. It may turn out to have been in the best interests of the United States and the hemisphere. On the other hand, it may not.

But there is no argument on one important point: the United States government kept the press from observing, first-hand, an important moment in the country's history, and the American people cheered. Not everybody, but the overwhelming majority thought that keeping the press out was a good idea.

I thought that's what we ought to examine tonight. And to give you a flavor of the public's attitude, I intend during my brief address this evening to read some exerpts from the letters I have received.

Letter #1
Fresno, California—"Dear John, ordinarily I would ignore what you said about the President curbing the press, but I think you should know where I was when I heard you. I was at my golf club with a scotch and soda in my hand, along with about

fifty other guys. When you said what you did about the administration doing things behind the back of the people, some guy yelled, "Well, you dumb bastard, what do you think we elected Reagan for? It's damned sure you were never elected."

Letter #2
From a minister who prepared a sermon defending the press in Waynesboro, Virginia: "I was sure that no one would take offense if I defended the Constitution and its guarantees of freedom of the press. I was wrong. In a gathering of our officers yesterday evening, I found that there is a strong feeling against the press. There is an anger that would deny the press the right to cover wars because of the coverage in Vietnam. They were angry at seeing so many wounded. They were angry at seeing the My Lai massacre. In their anger, they seem willing to deny the press, and themselves, the basic rights that are guaranteed in our Constitution."

Those two letters represent different points of view, but they both accurately reflect the mood of the country.
 Who elected the press?
 The answer, I think, is that the people who wrote the Constitution elected the press. It is more than just the First Amendment; the framers of the Constitution were explicit in their belief that the way to keep the United States free was to keep its press free.
 In another way, nobody elected the press and that's the way it should be. The press is not part of the political process. Journalists are not politicians. The press represents different points of view. What makes this a free country is that its citizens have access to those different viewpoints.

Letter #3
Grand Rapids, Michigan: "I am a moderate, sir, but I consider our government to be the representatives of the American people, be they embodied in our diplomatic corps or in the U.S. Marines. If we don't agree with the administration's policies, we vote them out."

But on what basis do we vote them out? On what information does an electorate depend for its judgments on any administration? There was a widespread belief in this country that the Johnson administration wasn't telling the whole truth about Vietnam, although in my view there was an effort to tell the truth in Vietnam. Mr. Nixon certainly didn't want certain things made public about the Watergate scandals. The Kennedy administration just lied about the Bay of Pigs.

I don't believe the press caused Lyndon Johnson not to run for reelection; he was struck with a tragic policy in Vietnam and he knew it. I don't think the press was the factor that caused Mr. Nixon to resign; he was about to be impeached, and he knew it. But in both of those cases the press played a role, for it was through the press that the people were able to make their own judgments.

Letter #4
Austin, Texas: "I fully believe the surprise element in the Grenada invasion of the multinational forces saved many lives—the Grenadians, the students, and the military personnel. Giving the press advance notice of this operation would have jeopardized these people."

Well, my understanding is that the United States government notified the governments of both Cuba and the Soviet Union before it invaded Grenada. One of things that we might have assumed, given the advance notification to the Cubans and the Russians, is that the Grenadians themselves might have known that something was up. The newspapers in the eastern Caribbean were filled with it, the British Sunday papers had the story, but it was kept from the American people and the American press.

Letter #5
Lima, Ohio: ". . . completely free coverage even at this initial crucial point in military tactics is in error."

John Chancellor

U.S. military personnel after the invasion of Grenada riding past what was Grenada Police Headquarters in St. George's.

The struggle between the press and the government over the invasion of Grenada has really nothing to do with "completely free coverage." There is a tradition in this country and in most of our sister democracies that when an invasion is planned, the press is "given advance notice."

Here's how that works.

When a country is planning to invade another country, a military operation requiring thousands of troops, the military authorities, the ministry of defense, or the department of defense, make up a pool of reporters and camera people, often only 15 or 20.

Private Wars: The Government and Press Censorship

Pool reporters are responsible to both colleagues and employers. Radio pool reporters share their reportage and their audio tapes with other radio reporters. A pool cameraman shares film or videotape with photo agencies or other networks. Newspaper poolers (as these reporters are called) share their notes and observations with other newspaper people.

A pool reporter is a representative of the press, who is obliged to share information with the press.

Pools are made up when there isn't room for everybody to go along on the story. It's an old practice. The White House press corps would be impossible to handle if everybody got to go to everything on a presidential trip, so the press is divided into pools. Those members of what we might call the invasion pool, which could have happened in Grenada, are told to pack their bags, but they are not often initially told where they are going. And when they are transported to the scene of the fighting, they are supervised by the military which also controls all the communications.

Generally, but not always, they are not among the first to land on the beach. But they are there soon enough after to do their work; they see the fighting. And only then, when surprise is no longer a factor, are they allowed to file their dispatches and send back their pictures. In wartime, a further point of control is added through field censorship. Nobody in the press wanted the American government to announce the invasion of Grenada in advance. The press wanted access to the story with the understanding that surprise and secrecy would be maintained. That not only saves the lives of military personnel, it also saves the lives of the press.

One pool reporter in Grenada—one—would have been enough. We would have complained bitterly about only one, but one pool reporter in Grenada would have preserved this ancient and honorable American principle that there are independent observers when the government is engaged in historic operations.

The press is less hostile to censorship and to the safety of troops than our critics believe. During World War II, when

John Chancellor

Edward R. Murrow, perhaps the most noted war correspondent of his time, in London.

Edward R. Murrow was broadcasting live from the rooftops of London during the blitz, he had a military censor standing at his side. If the censor thought that Murrow might be heading into an area of sensitive description of what he was reporting, the strength of the searchlights or the location of anti-aircraft guns, he would tap Murrow on the wrist and Murrow would start talking about something else.

Private Wars: The Government and Press Censorship

During the Second World War, General George Marshall, the Army chief of staff, had regular briefings for the senior editors and columnists in Washington. He would call them in, sit them down, and tell them absolutely everything. There was never a disclosure. The only thing he didn't tell them was the actual date of the Normandy Invasion. But General Eisenhower shared that vital piece of information with the pool reporters assigned to his headquarters in England.

Some will say, but that was the Second World War; the press is less trustworthy today. Yet, in 1980, when the Iranians were holding Americans hostage, a number of us in the press learned that in Tehran, a few American diplomats had managed to get out of the embassy and were in hiding in a friendly embassy in Tehran. That story wasn't printed or broadcast until the Americans got out of Iran. There was no disclosure in 1980.

Letter #6
Elizabethtown, Pennsylvania: "Surely when you talked about censorship you must have understood that within one or two days the media would have access to all the news that was necessary."

Two days after the invasion, 15 press people were allowed on Grenada under close supervision for only a few hours; three days after, 24 were allowed only during the day; four days after, 50 were brought in during the day. That may sound good, but the problem is that the significant events in Grenada took place during the first two days when there was no press allowed on the island.

Had there been television crews on the island during those first 48 hours, the American people would have seen pictures of American dead and American wounded, but the public would also have seen pictures of brave American soldiers in combat. My guess is, considering how popular the invasion has become with the public, the administration would actually have strengthened its case by letting the press be in at the beginning. Those pictures might have been a day or two late, but they would have had a powerful effect. By keeping the press out, the administration weakened its case, and even the Republican-controlled Senate passed a resolution by 53 to 18 asking that press restrictions be halted.

Letter #7
Glendale, Arizona: "Oops, John, you forgot to mention that President Carter didn't include journalists when he sent troops to try to free American hostages in Iran. Didn't President Ford leave journalists off the boat when he sent Marines to take the Mayaguez from the Cambodians?"

Quite right. Both the rescue attempt in Iran and the battle for the Mayaguez were rescue operations. They had to be done in a hurry and there was no time to assemble a press pool or even a single representative of the press. The point in these cases is that nobody in the press or in the Congress complained that the press was excluded. One was a highly secret desert mission in which every seat was needed operationally; the other was a response to a surprise pirate raid. In Grenada, the United States sent 6,000 troops ashore with plenty of time to assemble some press pools. Incidentally, I'm sorry that the press wasn't present in the Iranian desert or at the Mayaguez fight, because there are still arguments and disputes about what really happened in those cases. An observer from the press might have been able to set the record straight.

Letter #8
Concord, Ohio: "Did the Israelis include you on their mission to Uganda to Entebbe?"

No, but that was another rescue mission. The Israelis did not take pool reporters and camera crews. It was such a swift in-and-out raid, a commando attack, that there was no room for the press. But on Grenada, it wasn't that way at all.

Letter #9
Toledo, Ohio: "President Truman did not call in the press in advance of the bombing of Hiroshima or Nagasaki. . . . "

Private Wars: The Government and Press Censorship

There was no representative of the American press at the bombing of Hiroshima, but there was a member of the press aboard the plane which dropped the bomb on Nagasaki. The American government wanted an outside observer to be there, and a distinguished science reporter for the *New York Times*, William L. Laurence, rode in the plane and watched them drop the atomic bomb.

Letter #10
Troy, New York: "The media did not accompany the Bay of Pigs Invasion."

Well, a reporter who might have been assigned to that pool says, "Thank God!" But some publications knew part of the story and did not run it. The *New Republic* had part of the story and didn't run it when asked not to by President Kennedy. The *New York Times* had a good part of the story, and, again, didn't run it at the request of the President. Elements of the story did get out and that infuriated John F. Kennedy. Kennedy had good relations with the press, but the Bay of Pigs was not only a military disaster, it was an informational debacle. Among those who were not told in advance were Pierre Salinger, Mr. Kennedy's press secretary, and Adlai Stevenson, his representative at the United Nations.

Government press officers in the field were even worse. American reporters in Miami, once the invasion had begun, were told that an invading force of 5,000 was involved. Actually, only 1,000 had gone ashore, but the American press officers wanted the Cuban people to believe that a giant force had landed so they would rebel against the Castro government. Then, when the invading force got in trouble, the American briefers changed their story and said the force wasn't 5,000 after all, only a few hundred who had landed anti-Castro supplies.

Sometimes I think, as we all know, you can't believe your own government.

And, as most of us know, Kennedy later said to the *Times*, "If you had printed more about (the Bay of Pigs) you would have

British soldiers during amphibious landing training on Ascension Island. The soldiers were on their way south to join the Falkland task force.

saved us from a colossal mistake. I wish you had run everything on Cuba." Incidentally, the *New York Times* had advance word on the Cuban missile crisis as well, and again, at the request of President Kennedy, held up its story in the interest of national security.

Letter #11
Phoenix, Arizona: ". . . the British government did not make press access availability in a timely manner during the Falklands War. . . . The British government knew full well that the press had the power to make or break the success of the war through public sentiment after exposure of the horror of war through pictures. They remembered well from the Vietnam experience of the Johnson administration."

Private Wars: The Government and Press Censorship

That's true. When the Royal Navy Task Force was being put together to sail to the Falklands, the navy decided not to take any members of the press at all. Nobody. Prime Minister Thatcher insisted that the press go along, and a pool of correspondents and camera people was assembled—26, in all. (Not a large number, for a country going to war; the United States could have assembled a smaller pool for the invasion of Grenada.)

But the British government did take Vietnam into account, and every effort was made to impede and delay pictures going back to Britain. Television pictures, believe it or not, took two weeks to reach London, an amazing delay these days. An official of the ministry of defense told a friend of mine that the British government was not going to have homefront morale sapped by pictures of dead British soldiers on the telly every evening.

Vietnam haunts us all.

Letter #12
Leeds, Alabama: "It is doubtful that any government ever again will allow media coverage of a war, while it is going on, to the extent that such was permitted in Vietnam. There will always be reporters who sympathize with the other side or who, for one reason or another, oppose their own government's involvement in the conflict. If those people are allowed free reign in the war zone, especially with television cameras, they can have a devastating effect on the morale of our troops and of the people back home."

That raises some questions. Did the coverage in Vietnam have a devastating effect on the morale of our troops and the people at home?

The American government issued about 2,000 press credentials in Vietnam to American and non-American press. Only six were revoked because their holders broke the rules, and some of those were only temporary suspensions.

And for years in Vietnam the pictures and stories, especially the television pictures, didn't seem to have had much effect on either support for the war at home or the morale of the troops in the field. No war is ever popular with the troops, and Vietnam was no exception; yet the public opinion polls here at home didn't show a falling off of support until after the enemy's Tet Offensive in 1968.

Tet, in my view at any rate, was the great turning point of the Vietnam War, and pictures of that uprising did in fact have a lot to do with its impact. At that time in the war, before Tet, things were going well for the South Vietnamese and the United States. When the Tet Offensive began, it came as a complete surprise; main force and guerilla enemy units fighting all across South Vietnam, invading, briefly, the compound of the American Embassy in Saigon, capturing, for a bloody interval, The City of Hue.

Tet '68 was a tactical failure for the enemy. The South Vietnamese Communists lost so many people in that offensive that they were never again the decisive force in South Vietnam. Their losses insured that the North Vietnamese would henceforth run the show in the South.

But Tet '68 was a strategic victory for Hanoi. The pictures of our invaded embassy grounds in Saigon had a stunning impact here at home; so did the graphic coverage of the uprising in many South Vietnamese cities. The street fighting in Hue looked like World War II at its worst.

Tet made it look here at home as though the United States was up against a much tougher and much more resilient enemy than anyone, including the American military, had believed. The American government had accurately reported on battlefield success before Tet. After Tet, some senior American officials, including very senior uniformed officers, were stunned by the ability of the enemy to coordinate, in total secrecy, an attack of the size of the Tet Offensive.

While the American government was issuing press releases about the great failure of the Communists in the Tet Offensive, the Pentagon secretly and suddenly sought an increase in strength of 206,000 men in the armed forces. After Tet, in General Westmoreland's words to Washington, it was "a new ball game." The chairman of the joint chiefs of staff reported to the White House that Tet was a near run thing.

Richard Nixon was elected in 1969. The policy of vietnamization, turning the war over to the Vietnamese, began soon after. America's role in Vietnam had changed.

I go into this is some detail to counter a myth: the myth that the news organizations in Vietnam changed a defeat for the enemy in Tet '68 into a victory. What really happened is that the stories and pictures of that offensive were accurate, that the press reported what the press observed. The symbolism of the Tet Offensive was more important than the body counts. In its mindless way, the press coverage got the story right.

The press coverage of the fighting did amplify the psychological effect, the political effect of the Tet Offensive. But the American people were growing tired of that long war, and Tet made it seem as though that the war would have no end. Dean Rusk, then the hard-line secretary of state, talked about Tet many years later with Stanley Karnow, author of *Vietnam: A History*. Rusk said that his relatives in Cherokee County, Georgia, told him after the Tet Offensive, "Dean, if you can't tell us when this war is going to end, well then maybe we just ought to chuck it."

So I think it is a myth to say that the press got the Tet story wrong and unwittingly damaged the war effort. The press did what it always does: it reported what it is able to observe. And that goes to what we are discussing here tonight.

One of the best and most thoughtful books on Vietnam was written by Harry G. Summers, Jr., a colonel of infantry who now teaches at the Army War College. It is called *On Strategy: A Critical Analysis of the Vietnam War*. He writes, "There is a tendency in the military to blame our problems with public support on the media. That is too easy . . . an answer . . . the majority of the on-the scene reporting was factual—that is, the reporters honestly reported what they had seen firsthand. Much of what they saw was horrible, for that is the nature of war. It was this horror, not the reporting, that so influenced the American people."

And there we have the heart of it: the reporting isn't the problem, the problem is the intrinsic horror of war itself. In earlier conflicts, the horror of war was filtered to the public through ministries of propaganda, softened by censorship, delayed by slow technology. That is not true in today's world of instant communication. War reported by quill pens was more bearable to the folks at home than livingroom wars brought to us on videotape by satellite. And we have been learning that when civilians at home watch the intrinsic horrors of war on their television sets they don't like what they see—parents, husbands, brothers and sisters and friends, get upset when they see the dead and wounded.

This is handled in the totalitarian countries by eliminating a free press. But for the democracies, which depend on an informed citizenry, it is a unique problem. How should a government deal with the public's right to know if that right to know erodes the support the public gives the government?

Some of our most respected democracies have been turning to forms of censorship as an answer: Great Britain, Israel, the United States. We might not be surprised if this had been done in the Philippines or in South Korea, but it's being done, democratically speaking, in the best places. And it is being done, here at home, at a time when some of our fundamental attitudes about war, the public, and the press have been changed.

The United States no longer declares war. It didn't in the Korean conflict, in which almost 8,000,000 Americans served and 54,000 died; it didn't declare war in Vietnam, a conflict in which almost 9,000,000 Americans served and 58,000 died.

The Constitution says the Congress "shall have power . . . to declare war." The fact that over 100,000 Americans died in two undeclared wars helped cause the Congress to pass the war powers resolution, which restores some war-declaring power to the legislative branch—but since the passage of that resolution, every president has opposed it. Declaring war in this country has gone out of style.

Yet, a formal declaration of war has some advantages, not the least of them being that unless there is clear justification for

Private Wars: The Government and Press Censorship

a war, the Congress will not declare it. One of those advantages is censorship of the press. Censorship is not a pleasant experience for the press, but when it has been legally invoked by the American government it has, in the main, been fairly administered and obeyed by the press. Censorship in World War II, when it was last in effect, gave the public a reasonable picture of the war.

Could the American government and the American press agree today on an arrangement which would satisfy the government's requirements of security, secrecy, and surprise, and the press's requirements for access to the story, within bounds, while it's happening?

That might not be easy. It would be extremely difficult in places like Lebanon, where the press comes from many countries, some of them hostile to the United States. It would be hard to do in Central America. But it could be arranged in cases where American reporters and camerapeople are covering American forces. Grenada is such an example, and it could have been easily arranged there.

The chairman of the joint chiefs is setting up a panel of the military and the press to look into all of this, and we can only wish it well. But I was thinking about this today and I decided that the American government is to me the way a dentist is to a reluctant patient. They have just against my will pulled one of my teeth. And now they are going to have a panel to see if again against my will they can pull another tooth, and it seems to me that's not fair. I think we ought to go back to basic principles. The military, more than many civilians think, understands its relationship with the press, and in my view (the curiosities of Grenada notwithstanding) the military has behaved well toward the press. We may be an irritant, but anyone who went to West Point or the Naval Academy fully understands our responsibilities and our place in American society.

The fact is, we all need one another if this system of ours is going to work. The government needs the support of the public; the military needs the support of the public; the press, if it is to serve its function of independently informing the public, needs the cooperation of the government and the military.

Things get dangerous in a country when the government takes unto itself the function of informing the public. It is dangerous because every government likes to put its best face forward, and because no government likes to admit its mistakes. When your friendly government press agent, military or civilian, is your only source of information, you have to be worried.

A free press is, by definition, imperfect, contradictory, and inefficient. But it is infinitely preferable to a flow of information which comes solely from your government. America may not declare war anymore, but uniformed Americans are still being killed overseas, as we have seen recently in both Lebanon and Grenada. In Lebanon, there was nothing the American government could do to keep the public from being exposed to the horrors of war, as it affected Americans. In Grenada, it was possible to keep the deaths off television, and that decreased their impact from the visual and reduced it to the statistical.

Government policy in Lebanon is unpopular; government policy in Grenada is popular. For any government in the world, that's a lesson. For citizens of the democracies, it is more than a lesson, it is a warning of what may happen in the future.

5

Absence of Malice: Libel as Press Censorship

November 15, 1984

Perspective _____

The issue of libel is one that has long plagued journalists in both print and broadcast media. Former Time, Inc., editor in chief Henry Grunwald, a long-time defender of press freedom, speaks in this Fifth Annual Chet Huntley Memorial Lecture about the increasing threat that libel suits present to the cause of free and responsible journalism. Considered by many to be a serious infringement on the First Amendment right to press freedom, libel suits escalate in cost and damage to news organizations each year. They instill fear in journalists, making attempts at objective reporting a possible risk—one that reporters are less and less willing to take.

Grunwald, at the time of his lecture in 1984, was engaged in a particularly inflammatory lawsuit. Israeli Defense Minister Ariel Sharon had sued *Time* for $50 million in a libel suit. In a February 1983 cover story, *Time* had accused Sharon of "reportedly" condoning the violent massacre of hundreds of Palestinians interned at two refugee camps in Beirut, Lebanon. The defense minister shot back at *Time,* charging the magazine with "blood libel" and "anti-Semitism." *Time* ultimately won the case based on the precedent set in *New York Times* v. *Sullivan* (1964), which forgave possible judgment errors that demonstrate no "actual malice" or "reckless disregard for the truth." They won, to a large degree, because of Grunwald's unflinching belief in freedom of the press. But Sharon's charges badly scarred *Time* in the long run.

Certainly, journalists must be careful and respectful in reporting on public figures. Undue invasion into people's personal lives or propagating unfounded rumors is not responsible reporting. In all too many cases, however, responsible journalists are plagued by the looming threat of libel, which can cost millions of dollars in legal fees, in addition to damaging the reputation of journalists and publications. In our increasingly litigious society, libel, as Grunwald duly notes, has become "big business," with plaintiffs often demanding damages far exceeding necessary compensation. Such litigation, however, has as much to do with a widespread attempt to suppress journalistic freedom as it does with "the bottom line."

The First Amendment has been a fundamental tenet of the democratic system in the United States since the Bill of Rights was drawn up in 1791. In short, the article guarantees that "Congress shall make no law . . . abridging freedom of speech, or of the press." Yet this basic freedom is chipped away with each libel suit against a journalist's work. Grunwald does not deny that many libel suits are solidly grounded, particularly in cases involving the tabloid industry. The most lasting effect of libel suits, however, is to discourage journalists from reporting on the most important—often the most politically volatile—stories of the day.

Although the landmark *New York Times v. Sullivan* case, in theory, gave the media much greater breathing room than ever before, it has also left libel laws extremely hazy. The notions of "actual malice" and "reckless disregard for the truth" sound good, but are actually quite ambiguous, leaving the news media almost as vulnerable to libel attack as they had been before the decision. The term "public figure" has also been a point of contention. Is *anyone* in the public eye a "public figure," open to media probing, from the wife of a convicted murderer to a well-known senator? Grunwald's essay argues that the threat of libel at the drop of a hat has indeed become a form of press censorship, one that forces us to question the fundamental character of the Bill of Rights.

Absence of Malice: Libel as Press Censorship

Introduction of Henry Grunwald by Lawrence Grossman

Lawrence Grossman replaced Reuven Frank in 1984 as president of NBC News. A respected name in public television for many years prior to his NBC appointment, Grossman brought Tom Brokaw's "NBC Nightly News" to first place in the Nielsen ratings within a year of his presidency. He introduced Henry Grunwald, who delivered the fifth lecture in the Chet Huntley Memorial Series.

Introduction

I am particularly delighted to be able to introduce Henry Grunwald tonight, as a Chet Huntley Memorial Lecturer, because actually about the very first day that I came on the job at NBC News, I was asked to go down to NYU and serve, with the group, to select this year's speaker.

We quickly set up some very straightforward criteria for that speaker. It was clear that we wanted someone of superb intellect; someone of notable public accomplishments. We sought someone who would be a compelling speaker, and especially, in honor of the late Chet Huntley, someone who would have something significant and important to say about journalism.

Next year, we'll add two other requirements, I think, for the speaker. We'll want somebody who's libel-proof, and we'll probably want someone with trial experience. John Brademas, who is always working on behalf of this institution, was quick to add that it wouldn't hurt if we could find somebody who is a graduate of New York University.

And that, very speedily, narrowed the field down to one superb choice. Our speaker tonight, Henry Grunwald, of the Class of '44.

Actually, the fact of the matter is, Henry's professional life and his career path are not particularly interesting. It is one that my mother would admire greatly because, from 1944, when he graduated from NYU Phi Beta Kappa (he was editor in chief of the NYU newspaper; he majored in philosophy), he began working for *Time* magazine, and indeed has been with Time, Incorporated, ever since.

I say my mother would be very pleased with that career path because, when I came to New York looking for a job in 1953, I tried to get into *Time* magazine, was summarily rejected, and ended up with *Look* magazine. Three years later, when I decided that television was the wave of the future, I went to CBS. I called my mother, and I told her I was changing jobs, and she said I had committed an immoral act, that it was inappropriate and probably sinful—probably mortally sinful—to leave a company that was paying me every week to go somewhere else.

It was some years later, when *Look* folded, and I called my mother and I said "Aren't you glad that I left?," she said something that only a mother would say. She said "If you were still there, *Look* would still be there." And I think she blamed me for the magazine's demise.

Henry Grunwald, on the other hand, stuck with *Time* magazine. He began as a writer on foreign news, and he quickly became the youngest senior editor in the history of *Time* magazine.

The story is told about Henry that, when he was the youngest senior editor in the history of the magazine, he did some work on a cover piece about Albert Schweitzer. And he wrote some lines about Dr. Schweitzer's legendary arrogance. And at that point, an elderly and long-term religious researcher at *Time* came in shaking and wagging her finger, saying, "How dare you, a mere snip of a boy at 28, say anything like that about a saint like Albert Schweitzer?" And Henry was alleged to have said, "Madame, I am not 28, I'm 29."

Henry has been instrumental in some of the most brilliant innovations in the magazine world. *Time* magazine has evolved, as you know, continuing to stay up with the times and, indeed, be ahead of the times. He introduced the famous *Time* Essay section; he introduced the Environment section and the Behavior section; departments on the sexes and on energy; and he did the one thing that most endeared him to everybody that works at *Time* magazine under the editorial staff—he finally gave bylines to the writers.

Henry is the editor in chief of Time, Incorporated, which publishes many magazines; on the Board of Directors of the Book of the Month Club; but his interests are catholic and, indeed, diverse. He's the director of the World Press Freedom Committee, and has been very much involved in First Amendment matters and essays on the press. He's the director of the Metropolitan Opera Guild and a famous opera buff. And he's also the director of Scientists' Institute for Public Information, seeking to open light onto scientific developments in this country.

Henry is also very famous for being an editor who makes up his mind at the last minute, as many changes in *Time* magazine covers that have ended up in the trash basket can testify. And there is a needlepoint hanging in his office—in fact, I have a needlepoint hanging in my office—but the needlepoint hanging in Henry's office says "The editor's indecision is final." The one hanging in my office says "Our programs are chosen by fear, politics, pressure, and favoritism."

But I cite the needlepoint because Henry's advertised subject for tonight—as I'm sure many of you have seen on the signs around NYU—was to be "Nobody Loves the Press, and Whom Does the Press Love?" And today I received a call from Henry's office to say that he has changed his subject—that he plans to talk to us tonight about the very critical area now of libel.

It is a subject that I am delighted to hear about. We at NBC News, as many of you may know, have just won—fortunately—a long, onerous, arduous, and very expensive libel suit brought against us by Lyndon LaRouche in Virginia. Not only in that case had the jury found that our stories were truthful and accurate, but in the end they found for us on a counterclaim, and awarded $3,002,000 to NBC. I might say that the $2,000 were compensatory damages, and the $3 million were for punitive damages.

But Henry has, at the last minute, changed the title of his speech, as I say. He will talk to us on libel. It is a subject of critical importance in the whole area of the press, and of the First Amendment, and of our freedom, because it is a weapon that has been used—as I'm sure you all know—with great frequency and increasing danger, I happen to think, to the press recently.

Henry Grunwald

Born December 3, 1922, in Vienna, Austria, Grunwald emigrated to the United States in 1940 at the age of 18. After learning English through studies at New York University and frequent movie-going, Grunwald took a writing position at Time, *where in 1951 he became the youngest senior editor on the staff. He went on to serve as foreign editor, assistant managing editor, and managing editor of* Time. *When he took over (1979) as editor in chief of Time, Inc., which owns a number of magazines including* Time, Fortune, People, *and* Sports Illustrated, *Grunwald had already established a reputation as an astute judge of quality journalism who had the unnerving habit of making last-minute editorial decisions. In 1987, Grunwald accepted President Ronald Reagan's appointment as Ambassador to Austria. When he left that post in 1989, Vienna's* Daily Standard *spoke of Grunwald affectionately as "the son whom we drove out and to whom we owe so much." The author of biographical works on J. D. Salinger (1962) and Winston Churchill (1965), Henry Grunwald has always been an intellectual at heart. He is well-known for his constant, unflinching support of press freedom.*

Absence of Malice: Libel as Press Censorship

John Walter was an enterprising young editor who only four years before had started a paper that would become the *London Times.* One day he permitted a statement to be printed in his paper to the effect that the Dukes of York, Gloucester, and Cumberland had been insincere in their expressions of joy at King George III's recovery from an apparent mental breakdown in 1788. Walter was tried for libel, sentenced to a fine of 50 pounds and a year's imprisonment in Newgate. He managed to continue running his paper from what he called "this vile receptacle."

Such a story from the distant past evokes a certain troubling echo today. No, I do not expect, like Mr. Walter, to edit Time Inc.'s magazines from jail (although one never knows). I do not expect a return of the Star Chamber. I don't even expect a revival of certain ways of coping with the press that were popular in an earlier America, when editors were constantly in danger of being challenged to duels or horse whipped or beaten up by gangs. During the War of 1812, one antiwar newspaper was actually blasted by a mob with a cannon. On the developing frontier vigilantes shot up newspaper offices, and tarring and feathering editors was a popular pastime. Some of you may feel that those were the days!

Right now the press faces a different sort of threat, but again from libel. Indeed we are in the midst of a wave of libel actions and they have become a serious menace. That is especially true of libel suits brought by public officials who in spirit, if not in fact, sometimes seem to believe in the old English principle

Ariel Sharon after losing his libel suit against *Time* magazine.

of seditious libel which was, in effect, anything that offended the Crown or anyone else in authority.

Time, as most of you know, is currently in court defending itself against a libel suit brought by General Ariel Sharon. I won't say anything about that case except that I am certain *Time* will be vindicated. And of course you know about the suit by General William Westmoreland against CBS. It is significant that several right-wing legal activist groups have begun financing libel litigation against the press for political reasons. The head of one of these groups, Dan Burt, who is conducting the case against CBS, has said quite openly, "We are about to see the dismantling of a major news network." Obviously citizens have rights to redress if they are libeled; those rights must be balanced against the duties of the press. Our society is a delicate balancing act, in fact, an almost infinite number of balancing acts. The recent attempts to bash the press through libel actions suggest that, once again, there is real danger of the balance tilting against journalists.

Although recently the press has been winning 46 percent of libel cases that go to trial, which is better than in previous years, the average award in libel actions lost by the press has continued to be about $2 million. Incidentally, malpractice awards against doctors during a comparable period averaged under $700,000, suggesting that juries consider the press rather worse than bad medicine.

Among recent awards which stagger the imagination (not to mention the pocketbook) are: A $2.5 million judgment to a Texan who actually disavowed having suffered any injury from an erroneous statement in a book to the effect that he had been indicted for practicing optometry without a license. In fact, the wrong first name was used in an otherwise correct reference to his brother. The appeals court overturned the judgment. A far bigger libel and privacy award, $40 million, went to the writer Jackie Collins over a magazine's erroneous identification of her as an actress appearing topless in the movie version of her novel, *The World Is Full of Married Men*. In reversing this award, the appeals court said that the main publicity of the offending material came not from the circulation of the magazine, but from Ms. Collins' lawsuit and her own statements to the press.

There is also *Pring* v. *Penthouse,* another case involving both libel and invasion of privacy. Kimberly Pring, a former Miss Wyoming, was awarded $26.5 million in 1981 because *Penthouse* published a story about a fictional Miss Wyoming who caused men to levitate by performing certain sexual acts. In 1982, an appeals court overturned the verdict, which a judge had already reduced to $12.5 million.

All this is clearly out of proportion to any real damage suffered by the alleged victims. In fact, appeals or post-trial rulings so far have reduced or overturned all such megaverdicts. But sometimes a publisher doesn't have enough money to appeal. That was the case in *Green* v. *Alton Telegraph,* a small independent Illinois newspaper. A jury awarded the plaintiff $9.2 million, but the paper reportedly settled for $1.4 million.

Even when awards are reduced or smaller settlements are agreed upon, expenses are still tremendous. Trials go on for months and legal fees can amount to millions. In the Westmoreland libel case against CBS, both sides have spent more than $5 million just in preparation. Such awards, and such costs, are, in the colloquial as well as often in the technical sense, punitive.

What is going on?

Some people think it's just part of a growing American passion for litigation. According to Mayor Ed Koch, this explosion of litigation is partly caused by the explosion of lawyers. Some day, he suggested, all of us will be lawyers and we will earn our living suing each other. There is also the fact that juries and judges were not inclined to award large amounts of money in the past; it was not until recently that libel became big business.

One law professor with a bent for sociology has suggested that where the old-fashioned American remedy for criticism was a verbal counterattack or a swift punch in the nose, we now sue because in our society we have become obsessed with image.

Perhaps so, but I suspect that there is a simpler explanation which has to do with how the public, and public officials, feel about the press.

Libel suits by officials are not a totally new phenomenon. Teddy Roosevelt was enraged by charges in the *New York World* and in the *Indianapolis News* that corruption was involved in the purchase of the title to the Panama Canal and through his Attorney General, one Charles J. Bonaparte, he sued both papers. Of course he got nowhere.

American politicians generally have been far more thick skinned. As one California judge observed, Washington was called a murderer, Jefferson a blackguard, a knave, and insane, Henry Clay a pimp, and Andrew Johnson and Ulysses Grant drunkards. Lincoln was called a half-witted usurper, a baboon, a gorilla, a ghoul. Theodore Roosevelt was castigated as a traitor to his class, and Franklin Delano Roosevelt as a traitor to his country. Dwight D. Eisenhower was charged with being a conscious agent of the Communist conspiracy. And we must not forget the Cleveland-Blaine contest where an entire presidential campaign was waged on two bits of doggerel based on allegations that Mr. Blaine was dishonest and Mr. Cleveland had sired an illegitimate child—"Blaine, Blaine, James G. Blaine, the continental liar from the State of Maine," versus "Ma, Ma, where's my Pa? Gone to the White House, Ha! Ha! Ha!"

By comparison, some of the things that we print about our politicians today are downright sissy stuff. But I think our politicians and public figures generally are more thin skinned, more ready to sue, partly because the press is taken more seriously and is seen as more powerful than ever before. And here, of course, when I say the press, I very much include television news which has pervasive force undreamed of by Mr. Blaine from Maine or even by the imaginative Teddy Roosevelt.

Watergate was a turning point in this respect. By and large the work of the press in exposing the scandal was applauded. At the same time a lot of people began to brood about the fact that here was a case where the press, as they saw it, had deposed a president. Gradually a reaction set in. We of the press did not always make the situation any easier, because some of us tended to revel in our triumph. Many began to see us as arrogant and elitist and rather distant from our readers.

Since the seventies, one of the big controversies about the press has concerned its insistence on keeping sources confidential. Judges pour out subpoenas seeking to compel reporters to reveal their sources in criminal and other cases in order to help defendants (or sometimes prosecutors). The journalists argue that they have an absolute right to refuse under all circumstances. But by and large they prefer to risk jail and fines rather than sacrifice the principle of confidentiality, which is essential to our craft.

Many state legislatures have tried to uphold this principle by passing shield laws to protect journalists. These well-intentioned measures are probably useful in reducing the number of capricious subpoenas, arbitrary newsroom searches, and other forms of harassment. But the attack on the press seems to have shifted gradually from this issue of confidentiality to the much broader field of libel. In libel suits, of course, the question of whether sources must be named and under what circumstances is also often at issue. But the scope of the libel problem is obviously far larger. It may be slightly paranoid to say this, but one can almost hear a disembodied judicial voice pronouncing: "You don't want to reveal your sources? OK, we'll clobber you for something else—not just for where you get your information, but for what you print."

The modern law of libel begins, of course, with the *New York v. Sullivan* case, decided by the United States Supreme Court in 1964. As you know, the Court in the case for the first time held that libel regarding a public official—that is false statements of fact about such an individual which injure the individual's reputation—was protected by the First Amendment. The Court held that when a public official brings a libel action, he cannot collect damages for a defamatory falsehood unless he proves that it was published with "actual malice," meaning with the knowledge that it was false or with reckless disregard of whether it was false or not. Justice William Brennan wrote the opinion of the Court and he spoke of our "profound national commitment to the principle that debate on public issues should be uninhibited, robust, and wide open."

The facts of the Sullivan case concerned a civil rights advertisement appearing in the *New York Times* during a period of intense national stress. L. B. Sullivan was a city commissioner in Montgomery, Alabama, who objected to the ad, which cited certain actions by the police against black students and against Dr. Martin Luther King. Since everybody in Montgomery knew that he had responsibility for the police, Sullivan claimed that he had been libeled even though he was not named. He supported his claim by pointing out that some of the statements in the ad were incorrect. The local court in Alabama found the *Times* guilty and imposed a half million dollar libel judgment, the largest then on record in the state.

It must be remembered that the case had great political significance. The civil rights struggle was in full swing. The national press and TV played a big role in publicizing that struggle and were, therefore, resented if not hated in many quarters. The effect of the libel action was clearly to make an example and to frighten off the press. So the key to the *Sullivan* decision, which overturned the lower court ruling, may lie not in just the commitment to "uninhibited, robust, and wide open" public debate, but on the enunciation of that commitment on a *national* scale.

The central principle of *Times* v. *Sullivan* was already the law in the state of Kansas as early as 1908, and had been adopted by several other states before the *Times* decision. Eventually other states might well have adopted such a rule too. But in retrospect it seems evident just what the Supreme Court was up to; it was making certain that the emerging national communications media would be permitted to flourish rather than be stunted by the need to worry about particular libel rules in every single state. Only 400 or so copies of the *New York Times,* which then had a daily circulation of 650,000, went to Alabama, so it could not have been said that Alabama was an important source of profits for the *New York Times*. But the Supreme Court apparently felt that the ability of an Alabaman to receive what was in effect a national newspaper was of such importance that local libel rules had to yield.

I think we must pause for a moment over the *Sullivan* decision which has become so familiar but whose significance is really extraordinary. Frankly, many well-meaning people simply don't understand it. "If you print something wrong about a public official, why shouldn't he be just as free to sue you as anybody else?" That is probably how many citizens feel about it, even those who are not particularly antagonistic toward the press. And I can understand them. But the reason why public officials are *not* just as free to sue, without major qualifications, is at the heart of the *Sullivan* decision.

Put in lay language, it adds up to the notion that if any official could sue and collect for a falsehood, even one committed in good faith, the press would pretty soon be so intimidated, and perhaps so poor, that it might abandon or greatly reduce its role as a public watchdog. The lawyer and scholar who argued the case before the Supreme Court, Herbert Wechsler, in fact pleaded that the exemption should be absolute and that no public official should have the right to collect for libel for *any* statement concerning the performance of his duties. But realizing that this extreme position probably would not fly before The Brethren, he offered as an alternative the "actual malice" rule, meaning—to repeat—that a plaintiff can collect only for a falsehood that could be shown to have been published either knowingly or recklessly.

In accepting this argument, the Court obviously felt that public officials, as distinct from a private people, had a lot of opportunities to talk back and defend themselves. Moreover, public officials are privileged to say almost anything they want in the course of exercising their duties without danger of being sued. Thus, according to Justice Brennan, "it would give public servants and unjustified preference over the public they serve, if critics of official conduct did not have a fair equivalent of the immunity granted to the officials themselves."

Justice Brennan, some time after the *Sullivan* decision, linked this reasoning to a certain theory of democracy held by Professor Alexander Meiklejohn, an authority on free speech. Meiklejohn conceives of the First Amendment as the vehicle by which the citizens of the United States exercised sovereignty over themselves. Under his view, the people of the United States are not only "the governed," but also "the governors," and the citizen has not only the right to criticize official conduct, but the responsibility and the obligation.

Later the actual malice principle was applied not only to public officials but to "public figures." Chief Justice Earl Warren noted that, "Increasingly in this country, the distinctions between governmental and private sectors are blurred. . . . In many situations, policy [is made or carried out by] boards, committees, commissions, corporations, and associations, some only loosely connected with the government. . . . Many [individuals] who do not hold public office at the moment are nevertheless intimately involved in the resolution of important public questions or, by reason of their fame, shape events in areas of concern to society at large. . . . Our citizenry has a legitimate and substantial interest in the conduct of such persons, and freedom of the press to engage in uninhibited debate about their involvement in public issues and events is as crucial as it is in the case of 'public officials.'"

There has been a great deal of controversy about just who is and is not a public figure. A socialite divorcée who held press conferences during her divorce action was ruled *not* to be a public figure. On the other hand, a university athletic director *was* classified as a public figure. All this uncertainty is a serious problem to the press. But what I want to stress tonight is the role of public *officials,* and what has been happening as a result of the *Sullivan* decision in the last twenty years.

For a while the press seemed to fare very well. Judges almost routinely disposed by summary judgment of libel cases if they lacked merit under the "actual malice" rule. But then in 1979 Chief Justice Warren Burger wrote a footnote. It was part of a case in which a behavioral scientist sued Senator William Proxmire for giving the federal agencies that supported his research one of the famed "Golden Fleece Awards." His research, by the way, was on why monkeys clench their jaws. The footnote in effect told judges that henceforth they should go easy in rendering summary judgments in libel cases. Thereafter such judgments became much rarer and many more suits actually went to trial.

Justice Brennan has said that the press must have "breathing space," that is, the rules should be drawn to give the press the benefit of the doubt. Accordingly, the Court has suggested that "actual malice" could *not* be inferred just from the defamatory statement itself, nor from a publication's failure to retract, nor from an error in judgment, nor from a failure to verify facts before publication, nor even from ill will.

Sounds good. But the *tone* of Supreme Court decisions has been increasingly antipress. Also, many lower courts now seem to feel that, although none of these particular faults may equal actual malice, a *combination* of them may do the trick. In that view there is considerable danger for the press. Moreover, following what Theodore White in a different context has called the law of unintended consequences, the *Sullivan* decision created serious new problems of a different sort. Put very simply, it has not only opened up the newsroom, but the journalist's mind, to judicial inquiry.

If an editor or reporter has to prove that he did not print something recklessly and with disregard of its possible falsehood, what he knew and what he thought during the preparation of the story suddenly becomes a legitimate question. As Eugene Roberts, executive editor of the *Philadelphia Inquirer*, pointed out last year, lawyers are trying to confuse juries and are spending less time on what was in a reporter's story than what was in his notebook. "Jurors—most laymen for that matter—don't understand that in back of stories of a few hundred words are often thousands of words of notes and research. And plaintiff's lawyers are making it appear that in distilling the research down to a printable size, reporters are unfairly marshaling their facts and distorting them. The Catch-22 of all this is: the better and more conscientious the reporter, the vaster the research, and thus the greater the reporter's vulnerability to this line of attack from the plaintiff."

Nor do most laymen understand how a news story is put together. Any editor will tell you that an in-depth replay of any reporter's effort is likely to reveal factual inconsistencies and bias on the part of news sources (as news sources generally have an ax to grind), differing memories about exactly what was said and how, and similar ragged edges of all kinds. But that is a far cry from knowledge of falsity or recklessness.

Moreover, judges and juries, prompted by lawyers, have taken to scrutinizing news articles as if they were legal or theological documents, with sometimes absurd emphasis on words and even punctuation. In one notable example, a magazine reported on a set of stereo loudspeakers and noted that sound "wandered about the room" rather than "along the wall." That choice of words caused a jury to bring a libel verdict against the publisher, with an award of $115,000, a paltry sum nowadays. But the case cost many times that sum as it was fought all the way to the Supreme Court which finally overturned the judgment.

Nonjournalists also often fail to understand that doubts expressed about a story, or particular parts of a story in progress, do not prove carelessness or disregard of the facts, but often the contrary. Take the case in which the president of Mobil, William Tavoulareas, sued the *Washington Post* for in effect accusing him of nepotism. The jury's $2 million verdict against the *Post* was thrown out last year by the trial judge. But the jury had significantly been impressed by the fact that a copy editor had questioned the thrust of the story in a note to another editor. The *Post* got no credit for setting up a procedure that allowed the copy editor to be heard, only to be blamed for deciding, on balance, against the editor. Much the same can be said about the internal investigation conducted by CBS in the Westmoreland affair, an investigation now being used against CBS in court.

I can tell you from personal experience that editors and reporters have begun to think twice before writing notes to each other. They even sometimes hesitate over what they *say* to each other. Perhaps all this would be acceptable if it were to lead to greater care and a greater sense of responsibility. But in many cases it simply leads to caution and a tendency to shy away from controversy or risk. So an immensely important and benign ruling has greatly complicated our lives as journalists.

What if anything can we do about it? Many journalists feel that we should press for the absolute rule that nothing we report about a public official in line of the performance of his duty should be actionable—in other words, Professor Wechsler's original argument before the Supreme Court. There is a strong case for this, although it too might lead to unintended consequences. In this case the result probably would be pressure to carry more retractions. Well, there is nothing wrong with retractions as such when they are justified. But a legal or quasilegal requirement to use them in certain circumstances might violate the First Amendment, too. Anyway, the absolute exemption from libel for public officials is not likely to become reality anyway. So for the foreseeable future we will undoubtedly have to live with the "actual malice" rule—and, in fact, be grateful for it. We can only hope to limit its erosion.

One notion lies behind the current wave of libel suits and huge awards; the notion that the press is far too powerful. A few words need to be said about that. The image of the press as a colossus towering over society and government is profoundly misleading. Yes, the modern press has immense influence. Those who want to curb the press point out that it is no longer the "fragile" thing it was when the First Amendment was written. Well, neither is the government. Please consider the following. When Franklin Roosevelt took office, the federal budget, in 1984 dollars, amounted to about $54 billion. As you know, in fiscal 1984, it will be around $854 billion, give or take a few billion. When Franklin Roosevelt took office, the federal bureaucracy consisted of 600,000 people. Today it adds up to 2.9 million, President Reagan's best efforts to shrink the government notwithstanding. During Franklin Roosevelt's second term, the Washington bureau of the *New York Times* consisted of about 20 people; it has about 57 today. Numbers alone cannot express the relative size and power of government and press. But surely it is obvious that the growth of government has been far more dramatic, far more explosive than the growth of the press that attempts to cover it.

Armed with innumerable Xerox machines and printing presses and tapes and films, staffed with countless spokesmen and flacks, through tons of publications and reports awash with facts and figures, the government of the United States churns out enough information, and disinformation, to overwhelm any army of reporters. To find a story in all this that the government does not *want* you to find is a formidable task. Not that everything the government says should be automatically distrusted. We must continue to get over the Watergate Syndrome and must accept the notion that sometimes power is used benignly—even military power.

But we must also cling to our independent means of evaluation and judgment to keep a check on those in power. This applies not only to the government, but to many other large institutions—corporations, unions, foundations. After all, *everybody* tries to manage the news and to *use* the press, whether it's a political demagogue posing as a patriot; a pharmaceutical firm trying to pretend that some harmful drug is really a boon to mankind; or a rock star who was created by publicity, but complains of his loss of privacy—reminding one of Lillie Langtry's response when she was asked when the press would finally leave her alone. "Never, I hope," said Lillie. She was franker than most people who are happy to use the press, but are furious when they can't control the result. In the sense that the press must provide a platform for all kinds of opinions, even for the self-image of all kinds of people, the press *exists to be used*. But it must not let others dictate just *how* it is to be used.

I sometimes wish I could conduct an experiment. I wish I could take some judges off their benches, some jurors out of their enclosures, and give them a reporting assignment. Let's assume that we have heard a rumor about waste or corruption in the General Services Administration. Or perhaps we've had a tip about kickbacks in Pentagon procurement, or perhaps about illegal payments abroad by a large American corporation. Their assignment is to find out the facts. But suddenly, as they are playing reporter, the judge and the jurors are without the advantage of having witnesses summoned. They cannot hear them testify under the disciplines of contempt or perjury, or have documents produced under the compulsion of law. Suddenly they are without the benefit of having the case presented, for as long as necessary, according to an orderly and ritualistic system of evidence and argument. They are out there, to paraphrase what was said about Willie Loman, with a smile and a pencil. Well, maybe that's a little self-serving: most reporters these days have greater resources than that. Still, my hypothetical judge and jurors would have a pretty hard time fulfilling their assignment and getting their story. And what if they had to be afraid that an honest error, a misstatement by sources they trust, even some unforgivable but human error of theirs, could land them in a libel suit?

Please don't misunderstand me. Obviously I don't deny that some libel suits and some libel verdicts are justified. I even have some sympathy for Louis Nizer, who complained in a much noted column last year about reckless scandal sheets and the damage they do. Where Nizer is wrong, however, is in suggesting that the First Amendment should protect only publications that are respectable, by someone's definition, or that vulgar scandal is what most important libel suits are about. Incidentally, Nizer undertook to describe the victims of libel: "One must . . . see in their bloodshot eyes their sleepless nights; meet . . . their children sullen with sudden maturity, ashamed to go to school." As Oscar Wilde said of Little Nell's death, "One would have to have a heart of stone to read [the scene] without laughing."

Forgive the levity. I don't mean to make light of the harm the press can sometimes do. I am not denying that the press can be careless, reckless, unfair—as the Founding Fathers well knew. I am not denying that we have faults and are subject to hubris. During the Middle Ages in England, defamation was considered a sin and dealt with in ecclesiastical courts; it was punished with penance. I dare say there are times when some of us should be doing penance. But I also assert that the American press today, for all its shortcomings, for all its constant need to improve, is better and more responsible than it has ever been.

I do not believe that we should wrap ourselves in the First Amendment at every challenge. Like our political leaders, we must have thick skins. Libel actions, when we look at them in perspective, are an achievement of a civilized society; they have replaced, after all, at least in most cases, a resort to weapons to defend a reputation.

But we must not allow libel itself to become a weapon against the press. The damage would be not to the press only, but to the country and to those who for all their misgivings, still rely on us to tell the truth.

When I look up from these matters, as it were, and visualize the world beyond our borders, I sometimes feel a stunning sense of wonder. Here we are arguing about how far a reporter may go in accusing a public official and what recourse the official may have in seeking redress. Here we are arguing about the nuances of fairness and justice, the fine calibration of privileges, the careful weighing of restraints.

Yet in most of the world all this would be fantasy. Few reporters would even dream of daring to write or say what ours do routinely. And, if they did, the result would not be a libel suit, but a broken press or a broken body. I will not tell you that I can prove with scientific certainty that democracy cannot exist without a free press, but I know of no dictatorships in which there is a free press. Truth in much of the world is what the government says it is, and the press in much of the world is the government's lackey and nothing else. Even compared to some other, Western democracies, as American journalists we enjoy a freedom that is truly breathtaking. It is a freedom that must be earned again and again through responsibility; but above all we must understand and we must make our fellow citizens understand, that this freedom does not belong to us, but to them. As Judge Learned Hand said in a somewhat different context about the First Amendment: "To many this is, and always will be, folly; but we have staked upon it our all."

6

The Image versus the Word: Good and Bad Television News

November 20, 1985

Perspective

The question of positive news as an important component of broadcast journalism is the one Diane Sawyer discusses in her 1985 lecture, the sixth in the Chet Huntley Memorial Series. Sawyer notes how often viewers complain that there is too much negative news on the air—wars, toxic waste, drugs, crime, and any number of other issues. Audiences begin to wonder if there is anything right with the world today. Not surprisingly, they express the desire to hear a little "good news" now and then.

The Image versus the Word: Good and Bad Television News

The "good news," in many cases, is the type of story traditionally assigned to female correspondents—the "soft," human interest story that airs after the "real" news is presented. The complaint about the lack of "good news" has been a particularly sensitive issue for Diane Sawyer, who has never been known for backing out of a "hard" news story. As she herself has noted, "I love doing the 'boys' stories. . . . I probably do more Third World-jungle-slog-it-out-sweat-it-out-travel than anybody else here. I'm notorious for it." Striving to counteract the stereotype that women exclusively cover the human interest pieces, Sawyer has often had to prove herself through just the sort of "bad news" reporting that makes audiences wonder if there is a pessimist at the head of every major television news station.

At the time of this lecture, Diane Sawyer had been a correspondent with "60 Minutes," a show with a reputation for hard-hitting, investigative reporting, for just over a year. Correspondents on the show—Harry Reasoner, Morley Safer, Ed Bradley, and Mike Wallace—ran stories that were about as far from lightweight human interest news as one could get. Sawyer gained a reputation for using interviews as a forum for understanding current events. There was even some *good* news—such as the success stories of novelists Saul Bellow and William Kennedy. But Sawyer also reported her share of bad news. Indeed, her first story on the show was an interview with convicted murderer Velma Barfield, who was to be the first woman executed in the United States in over 20 years.

A contributing factor to the good news/bad news dilemma is the very nature of television. It is a medium that relies on images, so there is always the danger that television journalists will let striking pictures and videotape lead the story. The most striking, disturbing images, by and large, come from the bad news stories. Were the repeated airings of the Rodney King beating or the explosion of the Branch Davidian compound in Waco, Texas, examples of solid journalism, or were they irresponsible journalism based on sensational images? The key, says Sawyer, is to let the words lead the images, so that the story is kept in perspective. Clear, word-based reporting will ensure that the news, good or bad, will be presented responsibly.

As Sawyer points out, responsible television journalists must deliver the bad news. Is it not better to know that the foundation of a building is crumbling, so that it might be fixed, rather than risk the collapse of the entire structure? We might recall what Fred Friendly said in his 1982 lecture in this series. This is a dangerous world we live in, and "What we don't know *could* kill us." As important as it is to hear inspiring news—to assure us, now and then, that the situation is not hopeless—it is crucial for television journalists to let the American public know about society's ills. Only then can we work towards change.

The Image versus the Word: Good and Bad Television News

Introduction of Diane Sawyer by Lawrence Grossman

> *Lawrence Grossman replaced Reuven Frank in 1984 as president of NBC News. A respected name in public television for many years prior to his NBC appointment, Grossman brought Tom Brokaw's "NBC Nightly News" to first place in the Nielsen ratings within a year of his presidency. He introduced Diane Sawyer, who delivered the sixth lecture in the Chet Huntley Memorial Series.*

Introduction

*M*y job is to introduce Diane Sawyer. I did that last year, as you may recall, for Henry Grunwald, who is the editor of *Time* magazine, who was last year's Chet Huntley Memorial Lecturer, and I suppose—in the interest of equal time—I'd like to read to you an excerpt from the March 14, 1983 issue of *Newsweek* magazine.

Newsweek said, "By the testimony of professional colleagues and media critics, Diane Sawyer is brilliant, magnetic, industrious, inquisitive, disciplined, witty, gracious, charming, and loyal. And those," continued *Newsweek,* "are only half the compliments at hand." I certainly can't imagine what the other half of those compliments could have been. You don't hardly hear such gracious words about television journalists in this day and age.

But despite Diane Sawyer's meteoric career in television journalism, I have to tell you that she made one very major mistake. It's a big one. She went to work for the wrong damn network.

Diane has had excellent training in journalism. She was the editor of her Kentucky high school newspaper, a credential I emphasize because I, too, was an editor of my school paper (not in Kentucky, but in Brooklyn). And the only difference between us is that, with me, that editorship for the school newspaper was probably the one legitimate credential that I could claim in becoming president of NBC News.

Diane was also (and I say this in the interest of presenting the full picture) America's Junior Miss in 1963. She is well-educated—a Wellesley College graduate—and, in what I consider to be a move that shows very good judgment, Diane went to law school and dropped out after one semester. I say it shows good judgment not only because I also dropped out—although it took me a year to wise up—but because lawyers

The Image versus the Word: Good and Bad Television News

these days seem to rank even lower than journalists. And I think she's serving the nation a lot better as a reporter than as a lawyer.

Diane got her start in television, believe it or not, as a weathergirl—not a weatherperson, but in those days, a weathergirl—at station WKLY-TV, in Louisville, Kentucky. She became a part-time reporter for the station, and was quickly promoted to local correspondent.

In 1970, Diane moved to Washington, where she became the White House press assistant. She stayed with Richard Nixon for eight years—three of them in San Clemente, helping the former President to work on his memoirs. There, as Diane has said, she learned a lot about self-discipline and self-renewal.

In 1978, Diane made the mistake of joining CBS News, starting as a general assignment reporter and quickly earning her spurs on the Three Mile Island story. She moved over to the State Department, where her distinguished reporting of the Iran hostage crisis caused a lot of folks to pay a lot of attention very quickly. From there, she assumed the coanchor role at "CBS Morning News," where Diane, I must say, did me a great personal and professional favor.

Before I came to NBC, Diane left the "CBS Morning News" for prime time—for "60 Minutes." And Diane's departure from "CBS Morning News" undoubtedly was at least partially responsible for clearing the way for the "Today Show" to climb back up in the ratings this year. By joining "60 Minutes," she gave "Punky Brewster" and our entertainment division's Brandon Tartakoff a headache on Sunday nights at 7 o'clock. Which, I've got to tell you, is a lot better than me having the headache first thing every morning.

By the way, speaking of the "Today Show," I think I would use this public forum to deny a report appearing in today's *New York Times,* which was from Geneva, and talked about a press release that was circulated through Geneva, that warned of American agents who, quote, "kidnap innocent people—journalists, ballerinas, chess masters, and shepherds—drug them into submission, force them to accept huge sums of money, and, at gunpoint, make them appear on the "Today

Show." We are very competitive, but our own journalistic guidelines do not allow us to bring anybody on the show at gunpoint, although when you see some of the people, you wonder.

When Diane came on board "60 Minutes" as the series' first woman correspondent and coeditor, my friend, the series' executive producer Don Hewitt said, "I would have hired her even if her name was Tom Sawyer," which I think is a dopey thing to say since I can't imagine Diane's parents giving her a name like Tom.

In the last month, Diane has chiefly distinguished herself for two things: her exclusive interview with Egypt's president, Hosni Mubarak, after the Achilles Laural hijacking (NBC News caught Mr. Mubarak going into a car during the crisis, and we had him on "Nightly News," but I've got to tell you that Diane Sawyer's extended interview on "60 Minutes" gave us fits). Diane also made something of a mark this month by joining Don "T-Bone Pickins" Hewitt and then Carl Iconrada in their well-publicized effort to buy CBS News from the network. Needless to say, the idea of producers and correspondents buying a network's news division gives people like me pause. Someone suggested that it would be sort of like letting the inmates own the asylum (I didn't say that).

Well, CBS News is not for sale, we are told, and I'm glad for it, and I'm glad Larry Tisch got there first with more money. But now it is my great pleasure to introduce to you the brilliant, magnetic, industrious, inquisitive, disciplined, witty, gracious, charming, and loyal CBS News and "60 Minutes" correspondent and coeditor Diane Sawyer.

Diane Sawyer

Born December 22, 1945, in Glasgow, Kentucky, Diane Sawyer got her start in broadcasting as a weathergirl and part-time reporter at a Louisville, Kentucky, television station in 1967. She moved to Washington, D.C., in 1970 and joined President Richard Nixon's press office, advancing quickly to the position of speech writer. After Watergate broke and Nixon resigned, Sawyer remained with him for three years, assisting him in the preparation of his autobiography. In 1978, Diane Sawyer returned to Washington, D.C., where she landed a job as a reporter for CBS News. Sawyer covered such stories as the American hostage crisis in Iran and the Soviet military expansion along the Polish border in 1981. Her impressive work during the hostage crisis landed her a position as coanchor of "CBS Morning News." In 1984 she was named coeditor of the immensely popular "60 Minutes," becoming the first female reporter on the show. In 1989, Sawyer left CBS to coanchor ABC's "Prime Time Live" with Sam Donaldson. On the show, Sawyer has interviewed Russian president Boris Yeltsin from the Kremlin.

The Image versus the Word: Good and Bad Television News

I have to tell you—Larry Grossman told me the other day that when he was but a young boy, he would regularly, on a weekly basis, go into CBS News and ask to join Edward R. Murrow and his gang. And the whole time he was speaking just now, I couldn't help but think that if they'd had the foresight to hire him maybe—what do you think Andy (Rooney)—next Sunday night I would be saying, "I'm Diane Sawyer, those stories and Larry Grossman tonight on '60 Minutes.'"

It is a great pleasure to be here, a great honor to be speaking from a podium on an occasion in tribute to Chet Huntley, and to be succeeding the titans of journalism who have preceded me here. If I don't in humility keep demurring it's only because I'm reminded of a story that one of our fellow reporters, Tom Friedman, swears is true—that once a Washington envoy went to see Golda Meir, and went into her office and sat down, whereupon she paid him a compliment and he began to protest, and decline and demur and protest and decline, until finally she looked up at him and said, "Don't be so modest, you're not so great."

John Brademas does many things very well but it seems to me that one of the things he does the best and always has is to lock scholars and streetfighters in a room together and let them politely beat each other to a pulp. That way those of us who are on the streets and are not given much incentive for reflection get a chance to strengthen our muscles a bit by having to contend with larger ideas. And that way, scholars get a chance to be reminded just how dirty we fight when we really get down to it. That's the gift that John and the selection committee have given me tonight. They've given me a reason to test fly a theory or two, and a forum in which to do it in which I hope there will be relatively little damage either to the ideas or to myself.

I say that because I know that I have my nerve even venturing some of the things I'm going to venture, even trying to make some of the connections, because I know that there are countless of you in this room who know better and certainly know more than I do about these things. But if you will just indulge me, I will throw caution to the wind a bit and try to prove my mother wrong, hoping that you'll still respect me in the morning.

I hope you'll allow me to ruminate a bit on a question that I am often asked and I think most people in this profession are asked when they travel around. The question, of course, is that wonderful, hostile dumb-sounding question that you get every time that you go out on the road. Someone stands up and says, "Why don't you report more *good* news on television?" And I always say the usual things about what constitutes news, and blaming the questioner, the fact that we do put good news on and then cite one or two examples of goodhearted people doing good things. But I have, over the years, become less and less satisfied with my answer to that question, and I suppose I'm inclined to think it's because I've become less and less satisfied that that question is indeed the question that is on the mind of the person asking it. I'm just not convinced that the person asking that question is really concerned about the quantity of good versus bad stories on the air. I'm not convinced that beneath the hostile sounding query is a more fundamental concern, and maybe it can be phrased, perhaps too simply, as a question of whether we in television news still really believe in the possibility of progress in this country.

And the more I thought about it, the more it seemed to me that there are possible connections between the concern for the idea of progress outside the newsroom, in the livingroom, and our own concern, inside the newsroom, for the seriousness and the literacy of what we do on the air.

The Image versus the Word: Good and Bad Television News

A fine scholar and a friend of mine named Richard Landis at Columbia University was telling me the other day about a school of historians, French historians, who call themselves the school of "Longue Durée," and they call themselves that, as I understand it, because they believe that basically the way we're taught history in our high schools is fundamentally wrong, that we are taught to learn about dates and events and dynasties and crises and inventions, when in fact what matters are not the inventions and the events but how they are absorbed by people over the long duration, and how that absorption tells you so much about what people value at any given time. For instance, they think it's fairly silly to try to date the invention of the wheel when what matters is how different civilizations have used the wheel according to their idea of what was important. They would say that the Magna Carta really didn't matter, that it is a whole issue of the proliferation of contracts during the Middle Ages. They might even say that it really isn't important that one day Don Hewitt and his gang decided to buy CBS News—or as Don Hewitt puts it, he decided to ride off without a horse. They would say, instead, that the more important thing is the sentiment behind the gesture and how much we'll all be laughing about it a hundred years from now. And they would say that it's not who invented television that matters, or when it happened, but how the phenomenon influences and is influenced by our ideas of what is important in Western civilization.

Before I try to tackle that question and its relationship to the idea of progress, let me just ask you to make a very quick trip with me way back to an event that is far greater than the invention of television, maybe the grandest of all inventions, the invention of the alphabet, after which it is, well, I guess the only invention you can say, without it being a cliché, that the rest was history. As we all know, there was writing before the Greek alphabet came along, but the symbols were cumbersome and so precise and so specific that they weren't much use for abstractions—for ideas. But with the Greeks came the writing system that exploded the opportunities for thought, much as Einstein's theory of relativity finally took time and space and matter out of their cages. After the alphabet, for the first time language and thought were bound together in a mutually reinforcing dance of love, and what a dance it was as the laws were first written down, and by being written down, prompted other laws because finally you had laws that more than one person could remember. Thucydides and Herodotus began their exhilarating process of, for the first time, really separating myth from fact. History was no longer simply oral tradition adjusted conveniently to accommodate reality and self-interest. History was now about to become unretractable written word and with history in hand people were liberated from the tyranny of present tense. The past began to matter, both for itself and as a gauge of how far things had progressed. And with all those recordable facts, science could start making better categories.

I have to say I was reading *Science Digest* the other day, and I wondered to myself what on earth Aristotle might have thought of what he launched, when I took a look at an article that was ordering things, and went on to tell us that a man sheds 600,000 particles of skin every hour, 1.5 pounds of skin every year, that man's heart expends enough energy each day to lift almost 2,000 pounds to a height of 21 feet, while lovemaking by two people generates enough energy to run all household appliances, including the lights, refrigerator, stereo, and bedroom air conditioner, for ten minutes. Aristotle might have had second thoughts, and if science became more scientific with the alphabet, could thought be far behind?

The great philosophers began examining the way people think and learn and, as Plato put it, providing a philosophy that could help you distinguish between the real and the imagined when you looked at the flickering lights on the cave wall. In the process, he began to draw distinctions between natural and supernatural, asserting the importance of ideas and therefore the human beings who have them, until as Robert Nesbitt says in his wonderful book, "Plato came to the conclusion that there is a plentitude in the world of becoming. The seed crystal for the idea of human potential, for progress, was planted."

I was in the Amazon recently on a story and a translator for one of the Indian tribes there told me that in the Suiruee lan-

The Image versus the Word: Good and Bad Television News

guage, the language of a culture that has no written word, the word for "to think" is the same as the word for "to be sad." And of course it follows that in a culture such as that time is always as it has been, without a written history there were really limits on the ability to see much of a future. Pleasure was defined solely in the present tense, enough to eat and a place to sleep, and thinking was a fairly useless exercise; thinking couldn't make that much difference. But even Plato himself, who prized philosophy above all else, worried about the written word because he felt that reading and writing were the things that we do alone and there is a danger in that—that dialogue was a better kind of communication, that you communicate warmth with words and also when the other person doesn't understand, you can clear it up immediately, right on the spot, just as it used to be when the chiefs passed their words on to the tribe, and the priests to their initiates, and parents to children. And Plato worried that writing would weaken the power of the memory, the mystic cords of memory, the communal memory that binds people together in shared tradition, the kind of memory that changes with the time. It helps ease a society's passage through the rough spots.

Jack Goody of Cambridge University wrote an essay about the consequences of literacy and he talked about the British experience in Kenya. When they got there they discovered that the tribes in Kenya could remember their genealogy back literally for centuries. They could remember them, so the tidy, ever-tidy British decided to write them down. Of course chaos ensued, because the tribes had always been adjusting their genealogies to ease their relationships with each other. But no more. A memory is malleable, but facts are fighting words. So Plato, even though he loved his shiny new toy, the old conservative elitist that he was, feared the consequences of cultural change, of too much writing, too much solitude, the passage from the Garden of Eden in which myths unify us, a passage which left us alone with our thoughts in the world.

And, of course, Plato was right. The written word did change things, but I expect if he could have had any idea, even elitist that he was, of what the written word, what literacy, was going to do as it barreled down the centuries, how it would embolden all of the people who mastered it, what it would do for their sense of independence and worth, then he would have changed his mind. What it did in the Middle Ages with the convergence of urbanization and commerce and the printing press and reading glasses, for that matter, universities and the first words in the vernacular. And then with this explosion in literacy, that other quantum leap forward in the Middle Ages, when the Catholic Church, I guess, finally decided it had been embarrassed once too often by running around and proclaiming loudly that the world was going to end and to say that in the modern parlance it was time to low-key it a bit on that question. They had pushed the date back to the year 1,000 and when it didn't happen, St. Augustine, who was convinced that the world was a *massa damnata,* a damned blob, effectively had to yield to the theologians who were ready to mortgage the spiritual future to the present. People started paying more attention to the possibility of improving things on earth, with literacy as one of the main tools in doing it. That seed crystal from the Greeks finally hits its supersaturated solution and starts to drench Western thought, and nowhere more than in this country, of course, where the credo was written by old Thomas "perfectibility of mankind" Jefferson himself.

And then something happened at the end of World War II. Several things happened, I suppose, in the postwar era. The bomb took over where St. Augustine left off. The possibility of the end of the world was back—a secular Armageddon. And then there was all that empirical evidence that progress had been stalled. Vietnam, Watergate, the anarchy of terrorism in Iran, pollution, the "Dukes of Hazzard," and into the mix comes television news with its powerful pictures reawakening the old tension between the preliterate and the literate world, the visceral world and the rational world, the passive world that is full of things that are observed and can't be changed in the observing, and the active world of words designed to make a difference. Some people argued that it was good because over the long duration that we would all end up sitting around the genial campfire in McLuhan's Global Village. And some

The Image versus the Word: Good and Bad Television News

people argued that television was eroding everything that we had gained over the years with literacy. And some people argued, were willing to argue, that in the best of all possible worlds, in the golden age of television news, you could have the best of the preliterate era—the pictures—and the best of literacy too; that the pictures could be used in the service of words and the ideas, including the idea of progress. I've always believed that one of the central defining distinctions of Edward R. Murrow and his boys was this—that they believed in the power of the word that they were using, they believed that the truth they told could actually change things. You can hear it in the passion and personality of the reporting and in what Ed Diamond tells us Fred Friendly said about Murrow—namely that what made Murrow the man we remember was the intensity of his conscience. You can hear it from Eric Sevareid who told me recently that—in the fine careless rapture of the new thing of broadcast journalism (and it was Eric who dubbed it electronic journalism)—he did believe that the natural by-product and, in some ways, the inspiring by-product of the reporting was that lives actually could be improved. Nor do I think that it was any coincidence that this was a spirit that prevailed easily in what has to be seen as the golden age of radio broadcasting, for radio was all about voiced words, the literate word conveyed more widely and, to be sure, with more emotional emphasis at times, but still basically broadcasting in control of the words. Nor is it any coincidence that in the early days of television you could find the belief in the power of journalism and progress, the frontier days when John Chancellor said that Chet Huntley was an early settler. David Brinkley said of him, "He feels a sense of involvement in the news, sometimes you can see that he's personally affronted by the news." Or, in Huntley's own words, "I've always believed that mass communication should aim just over the horizon, and especially television, because if you don't give people something to aspire to, how are they ever going to get there?"

I think it has something to do as well with the proximity of journalism even in the early days of television news to the thought and not the picture—in other words, the old relationship between literacy and the idea of progress was still intact. Nor is it any coincidence that a lot of our ambivalences in this business—where there are ambivalences, where they exist—have to do with a tug of war between our journalism and the pictures. Sometimes we feel as if we're reduced to tour guides who accompany the pictures, sometimes we even accompany them well, but we still know that journalism ought to be an activity of thinking people who refract events off of their own experience and education, that no matter how much the technology dazzles us and delights us, that in the end it ought still to come down to us and our words. To use Roger Rosenblatt's wonderful primary question of journalism that in the end it is the journalist who has to answer with the words, "What shall we make of this?"

So that, in a sense as we practice our craft today in television journalism, we are making choices for that long duration, and the choice we make either asserts the primacy of literacy so that the words still give us the philosophy by which to judge reality from illusion on the flickering walls of our electronic caves. And, in a larger sense, it's also a choice about whether we continue to believe that the words and the truth they reveal can improve the human condition. Don't get me wrong, I am not a Luddite about the visceral, emotional, even sometimes irresponsible, assault of the pictures on us. I don't even mind that they threaten the rigid purity of the dry fact, though I do think just as an aside that it's interesting—at least I draw this conclusion—that one of the reasons the president's lack of precision is sometimes unremarked by the public is the fact that the pictures on television make people think they know the truth about what he means despite sometimes the words he says and later has to correct.

I also believe that in some measure television and its pictures do restore that preliterate common humanity that Plato was so worried about; it does reduce a bit the isolation. Though, I hasten to add, we haven't figured out a very good means—and Larry Grossman made this point to me the other day—for accomplishing that other part of his worry, namely

The Image versus the Word: Good and Bad Television News

figuring out some way for the audience to clear up misunderstandings and to talk back. I also believe that there are times when we should just be tour guides for the pictures, but not often.

What bothers me is the sense that we are increasingly in a way cowed by our own inventions. Because of the power of the pictures, we no longer fully believe in the power of the televised word. We no longer insist—if we ever did—that journalists be trained a bit in the school of life, but also be trained to think and write and to use the word above all else. We are proud of John Chancellor, George Will, and Bill Moyers, but we're not convinced that the place for them is in television news. They aren't sure that our values and theirs are the same. We treasure the Kuralts and the Utleys, the Safers and the Reasoners, and the Ted Koppels, and the Andy Rooneys—the good writers—but we don't keep insisting that their words define what we really do at our best. And in the privacy of our editing rooms I'm not sure that there's a single one of us who has not at some time yielded to the power of the picture and let it lead the story when it shouldn't have. And, if that's not so bad, I expect we all have gone even further and let the picture suddenly decide what the story is.

The consequence is a lot more than just for individual stories and individual reporters, because I really believe that the further we stray from the primacy of the written word the dimmer our conviction becomes that our journalism—television journalism—can make a positive difference. Michael Arlen argued in one of his wonderful essays that the "tyranny of the visual" was robbing broadcast journalists of their passion and personality and, in an interesting way, if you read the piece by Maureen Dowd in the *New York Times* last Sunday it seems that in the art world something very similar may have taken place. I was struck by the parallels when one of her witnesses said that he had been fascinated to see what would happen to the art of a generation that was raised on television pictures and Andy Warhol. The answer, it seemed in her article, was that artists with a kind of preliterate belief that all things are malleable, illusions essentially, everything, one of them told her, is mar-

Diane Sawyer

Diane Sawyer and Mohammed Ag Albakaye, whom she had interviewed in a famine-refugee camp in mali in 1985. Albakaye, who was then malnourished and suffered from malaria, was adopted by an Indianapolis family. Here, Albakaye visited Manhattan with Sawyer.

keting. And only Larry Rivers pointed out that the difference between today and the 1950s was that back in the fifties he really believed that art could tell you what was wrong with the world—that art could make a difference.

Which brings me back to the question that launched this whole exercise—the question we are all asked repeatedly

The Image versus the Word: Good and Bad Television News

about the amount of good news we put on the air. Because I believe at the heart of the hostility of that question is the fact that by and large Americans still want to believe their original premise about the perfectibility of mankind, and they see us as not just negative, but as somehow assaulting this treasured fundamental American premise. To some extent it's true and will always be true and we're proud—it must be true because often the news is bad, and when it is, we're going to report it, and the more widely it's disseminated the more it challenges naturally the notion of progress. But there are other things in the industry that maybe we should take a look at a little more closely.

In part, it's a question of style. Does it go too far to say that viewers subconsciously know that sometimes we do yield more to pictures than we care about the words, and the less we care about the words the less we assert the hard-earned belief that human beings can change things. And in part it's a question of attitude, not that we should be advocates who believe we can make the judgments about the substance of progress, but that we should be actively wedded to the galvanizing neutral belief that the truth can make a difference, and that all those differences do in the end add up to progress. And maybe that belief, suddenly coursing through our words, that we need to restore some of the passion and personality that sometimes we think we've lost.

And, in part, it's a question of time, since the sense of progress requires that sense of history, of the past informing and motivating it. Will we ever take the time on the air to form the connections between the past and the present? And, in part, it's also a question of substance, and I realize that here I am treading on very dangerous ground. But I come back again to that aggressive question from the viewer. The television audience is not unintelligent. They know we put a lot of news on the air about nice people doing good things. They know we tell statistics that are often good or at least neutral. But I think they suspect—and I'm sure or I don't suspect that they are right—that we don't devote nearly as much zeal to the search for news of progress as we do for the search of some dramatic iniquity to expose. Michael Arlen says he thinks that's why the documentary is in trouble. He says that people don't see the documentaries any more as explorations of how far we've come and what's wrong and how far we still have to go, but they see them as punishments, as some kind of public flogging. What is the difference in the end between good news and news of progress?

Good news, as we most often define it, is soft—which as we all know isn't really news at all. But real progress is rooted in fact. If 50 hungry children are fed, the facts about how many have been fed, how they were fed, do pertain, even though another 50 may still be hungry. If there is disease to report, there is also news about the virtual elimination of, say, smallpox from the world. That, too, is a headline. I think that the hostile viewers, for the most part, don't really believe that we think that progress is possible and so they're frustrated that in a world of injustice and brutality and hardship we don't seem to give, sometimes in Chet Huntley's words, "people need something to aspire to."

I think it even explains that curious contradiction in part in the polls where people, when asked if we tell the truth, say yes, but when asked if we give both sides of the story, say no. It's not cockeyed optimism I'm talking about; it's just an attitude that entertains the possibility that progress is possible and maybe it's the kind of optimism that Bill Moyers always tells about when he talks about going allegedly to see a friend of his on Wall Street and saying, "What do you think of the market?" And the friend says, "I'm optimistic." And Bill Moyers asks, "Well, why then do you look so awful and glum?" And his friends says, "It's because I'm not sure my optimism is justified."

I can hear people say that the danger of this kind of talk is that it leads to the direction of Robert MacNeil's phrase that "we end up cheerleading for the side that has already won." But all I'm saying relly is that it's something that we should think about, not because it ingratiates us with the American public, that's not the point, but maybe just to think about our values and for our pleasure in what we do. Because I see a

The Image versus the Word: Good and Bad Television News

belief in progress firing up the drive to expose real injustice, dramatic and not so dramatic. Our province will still be, in Gay Talese's words, "the part of the planet marked by madness, riots and raids, crumbling countries, sinking ships, gloom and spectacle," but as we all know, it takes a tough mind to look at the grey areas, much tougher than the black and white.

It strikes me that just maybe we can have the pleasure of lighting a candle and cursing the darkness, too. And I see the belief in progress in the importance of good writing and that's the pleasure in the end, reinforcing each other so that the medium becomes the place for the powerful truth and powerful words over the long duration.

In preparation for this speech, as just a little exercise for myself, I decided to ask a few people what they think history will consider the golden age of television reporting. And what surprised me the most was how many people thought that all of the ingredients for a golden age are here. Don Hewitt and Ed Joyce both talked about the combination of air time and technology, and people with the skills of Koppel and Rather and Brokaw and Jennings. And how many of them talked about the need to reassert the seriousness of our journalism. Larry (Grossman) talked about the importance of the idea and the word. Tom Brokaw and Dan Rather both mentioned an hour newscast as a way to signal the serious writers and thinkers that there is room for them in television, and Walter Cronkite said that the networks must commit themselves to frequent hard-hitting documentaries so that we can do our job of holding up the mirror which paves the way for improving the human condition.

The thoughtful word, the idea of progress, and the opportunity of television all together awaiting a golden age, so that the words to close with have to be Chet Huntley's on his last broadcast on the "Huntley-Brinkley" report. "At the risk of sounding presumptuous, I would say to all of you, 'Be patient and have courage for there will be better and happier news one day if we work at it.'"

7

Choosing a President: Are Media Part of the Problem?

March 10, 1988

Perspective

In an earlier lecture from this series, Anthony Lewis spoke of the power—real or imagined—of the press in shaping the U.S. presidency. Indeed, the subject is one which many in America have come to question today, where "spin doctors" are as much a part of the fabric of presidential elections as party bosses once were. In his 1988 lecture, *New York Times* columnist Tom Wicker focuses on the campaign phase of the presidency and demonstrates how the media may be playing too large a role in the process, pushing the public—intentionally or not—towards decisions it might otherwise not make. Wicker points in particular to the primaries, a relatively new development which gives media representatives the power to decide which candidates, and indeed which primaries, are significant, and which can be ignored.

Wicker notes how the Iowa and New Hampshire primaries, because they come first in the series, have been deemed particularly newsworthy by journalists—not because either state is known to be especially representative of the American public, but because they come first in the series of contests. A candidate who emerges from one or both of these primaries in good standing has an excellent chance of later nomination, and will garner greater attention from the press as the campaign unfolds. Indeed, statistics estimate that New Hampshire receives at least four times as much coverage on the major networks as does the later New York primary—certainly not a minor affair—six weeks later. Strong candidates in recent elections, such as John Glenn, Bruce Babbitt, and Howard Baker, were essentially knocked out of the race after poor showings in the New Hampshire primary. From that time on, they were all but ignored by the press. Indeed, it is hard to dispute the argument that the press holds significant power to decide which candidates it likes best, and focus on those.

Few would deny that former president Jimmy Carter, along with 1984 also-ran Gary Hart, were largely created by the media. In both cases, it was good showings in New Hampshire and Iowa that brought them into the public eye. Gary Hart, a little-known Colorado senator, began his rapid rise with small articles on the political pages of the *New York Times,* and ended up on the covers of *Time, Newsweek,* and *People* magazines soon after the primaries began. And Carter, a former peanut farmer and one-term governor of Georgia, ran against such Democratic party heavyweights as George Wallace and Jerry Brown to win the party's nomination and, in his case, the presidency as well.

As Wicker argues, the media can ruin a good candidate in the space of two primaries, which are actually no more important than any of the others that follow. In essence, he suggests, the news media created the fanfare surrounding the New

Hampshire and Iowa primaries and, indeed, manufactured the very significance of the primary system. Never a requirement for candidacy, the primaries provide an opportunity for a candidate to gain press coverage, or risk losing it. The press, and its eager audience, "thirst for drama" in the initial stages of the primary process, as Wicker points out. In an age of politics that has been characterized by "sound bites" rather than substance, Wicker asks if media representatives are properly informing the American public, which looks to the media as its major source of information regarding presidential candidates.

Choosing a President: Are Media Part of the Problem?

Introduction of Tom Wicker by Tom Brokaw

A television journalist since 1962, Tom Brokaw began as a local reporter in Omaha, Nebraska. He worked his way up through the broadcast ranks, ultimately becoming anchor of the "NBC Nightly News," a position he has held since 1983. Brokaw has hosted a number of NBC News special reports. He introduced the seventh speaker in the Chet Huntley Memorial Lecture Series, newspaper columnist Tom Wicker.

Introduction

Our guest speaker tonight is one of America's best-known journalists—Tom Wicker of the *New York Times*.

Mr. Wicker is a son of the South, the birthplace of many distinguished American writers. Although we know him best for his *Times'* column, "In the Nation," he began life and his career in the cross-roads communities of his native North Carolina.

What better preparation for the august corridors of power in Washington and at the Good Grey Lady than serving as editor of the *Sandhill Citizen* or *The Robesonian* in Lumberton, North Carolina. And since life is also a sporting contest, what better credentials than serving as Sports Editor of the *Winston-Salem Journal*.

But a man of such obvious talents as a reporter, editor, and author could not be overlooked for long. In 1960, after working on the *Nashville Tennessean,* Mr. Wicker became one of Scotty's boys, a member of the Washington bureau of the *New York Times*. He was present at the creation of the New Frontier and present the day it ended in Dallas.

Tom went on to become Scotty's successor as bureau chief and one of America's premier political commentators with his column, "In the Nation."

He's the author of several works of fiction and observations on the American political process and no one is better qualified to speak to us tonight.

Tom Wicker

Born June 18, 1926, in Hamlet, North Carolina, Wicker graduated from the University of North Carolina and worked as a reporter for newspapers in Aberdeen, Lumberton, and Winston-Salem. He was named Neiman fellow at Harvard University in 1957, and the following year took a position as associate editor with the Nashville Tennessean. *After applying unsuccessfully several times to the* New York Times, *he was finally hired by the Washington bureau in 1960. He was named Washington bureau chief in 1964, and in 1968 he became associate editor of the* Times. *He retired from that post in 1985, but still writes his popular "In the Nation" column, which has been a fixture of the* Times *editorial page for more than 25 years. A prolific writer, Wicker has authored numerous works of fiction, from his early thrillers published under a pseudonym, to such bestselling political novels as* Facing the Lions *(1973) and* Donovan's Wife *(1992). His nonfiction works about the American political scene include* Kennedy Without Tears: The Man Behind the Myth *(1964) and* One of Us: Richard Nixon and the American Dream *(1991). A recipient of numerous journalistic awards, his articles have appeared in all of the major news magazines, in addition to the* New York Times.

Choosing a President: Are Media Part of the Problem?

*F*ifteen years ago, I published a novel about a presidential election that I imagined as having happened in the early 1950s. The main character, not unnaturally, was a political reporter and one of the other characters was a political boss named Dunn. We still had bosses in the 1950s.

At one point in my story, the reporter says to Dunn that he believes "a presidential candidacy begins . . . in 'the speculation.' All that gossip, insight, fact, fancy, prejudice, and propaganda that political writers like to pass on to the nation—which is just to say *our* sense of a situation and its possibilities."

Dunn replies: "Not a bad system. You guys are a sort of nominations committee acting for everybody else. You can't all be fooled all of the time and damn few of you can be bought. Your biggest weakness is that too many of you want to believe in people and things you're too lazy to question. But in my experience your committee does manage to weed out the culls. . . . I think political writers provide a pretty good test of whether a man's got it or not."

Well, if you expand the definition of "political writers" to include television correspondents—very few of whom were around in 1952—that passage is still relevant to the presidential politics we have now. The political writers of print and broadcasting are still a sort of nominating committee acting for everybody else.

The questions I want to raise tonight are whether they form a fundamentally different sort of nominating committee than they once did, and if so, whether that's an improvement. In short, could a reincarnated Dunn, brought back from the elephant graveyard of oldtime bosses, still say that "political writers provide a pretty good test of whether a man's got it or not."

Let's begin with the year 1968—an apocalyptic year in every way, but one particularly significant for presidential politics. After President Johnson's announcement that he would not seek reelection—still one of the great shockers of my experience—the Democratic party was bitterly divided, and not just between those for and against the war in Vietnam. The latter were further divided between those who supported Eugene McCarthy and those who followed Robert Kennedy.

But after Kennedy was murdered in June, McCarthy went into a kind of political coma. The way was therefore open for Vice President Hubert Humphrey to be nominated—which he probably would have been in any case, even though *he had not entered or contested a single primary.*

Humphrey, therefore, was seen as the minority choice of prowar, pro-Johnson Democrats, unfairly installed by the machinations of the President and men like Mayor Daley of Chicago and John B. Connally—then an affluent Democrat rather than a bankrupt Republican. That view was understandable if not entirely accurate, and opponents of the war in Vietnam felt disenfranchised within their own party.

After all, Robert Kennedy had won five primaries, including the big last one in California, and 30.6 percent of the total Democratic primary vote. McCarthy had done even better, winning six primaries and 38.7 percent of the primary vote. So together they won about 70 percent of Democratic primary voters. Kennedy's murder, moreover, made it possible for anyone to believe *he* would have been nominated had he lived. Many Democrats still believe that.

In that atmosphere, Kennedy and McCarthy supporters cooperated—though on little else—in establishing a party reform commission. Their aim was to "right the wrongs" (and there had been plenty of them) of delegation selection in 1968 by establishing rules for a new and open party in 1972.

That commission opened up the party all right, but as is usually the case with institutional reform, the consequences were not exactly as expected. First, the national party committee was given effective control over what had been 50 independent state parties. Then, stringent national delegate selection rules were laid down.

Candidates were to be awarded numbers of delegates proportionate to their support in primaries or caucuses. Adequate representation for blacks, young people, and women was required. Delegates had to be chosen in the year in which they would serve, which ruled out early state commitments to established leaders. Governors and other party leaders were barred from handpicking more than a small percentage of delegates. The unit rule, under which a delegation had to vote as its majority dictated, was banned. With some modification, these rules remain in effect.

Delegate selection and delegation control, in a nutshell, were taken out of the hands of state party leaders. State parties, faced with these mandatory rules, had to turn either to an open convention or to an open primary for the selection of state delegates. The result, even by 1972, was a proliferation of primaries.

In 1968, only 49 percent of delegates to the Democratic national convention had been chosen in primaries; by 1972, that figure rose to 66 percent—and 58 percent of delegates had been committed to vote a certain way, not by party leaders but by the results of primaries. This year, I believe, there are 36 state primaries compared to the 11 of 1968.

Who could be against any of this? I certainly wasn't, though I wrote a great deal about what was happening. The Democratic party, as I saw it, was being opened to the people; bossism was over. But other things were happening too. Let me leap forward here to 1972, and Richard Nixon's huge victory over McGovern—achieved, however, with the aid of numerous financial excesses. These led directly to legislation for the public financing of presidential campaigns, including primaries, and to limits on individual contributions to candidates.

State party leaders' influence in the nomination of presidential candidates already had been greatly reduced; the financing reforms took state parties largely out of another important role—fundraising. Thus were downgraded those who usually had put the most emphasis on "electability"—the ability to win—and the least on doctrinal purity.

As states fell into line with the new rules, candidates could put their own choices on delegate slates. Even coming in second or third in a string of primaries assured them a committed delegate bloc at the convention. Albert Gore carried North Carolina earlier this week. He got 41 delegates, but Jesse Jackson, coming in second, won 38.

That kind of result encouraged candidates to build up their own factional strength and it invited more candidates to enter more primaries—the more running, the fewer votes required to do well and win delegates. And delegate factions chosen by a candidate for their loyalty to him were bound to be less open to switching and compromising—dealing.

In some states, changes in the law were required to establish primaries, and in that regard, the Republicans were dragged along with the Democratic reforms. But Republican state parties remained more independent. For example, they can award all of a state's delegates to a primary winner, as Georgia did to George Bush last Tuesday.

That party, in any case, serves a narrower band of interests than the Democrats do. The larger consequence was that the Republicans were able to remain, or become, a more nearly national and coalition-based party, while the Democrats have sunk deeply into factionalism, which is really what's meant by talk about a party of "special interests."

That factionalism, perceived unfavorably by the general public, resulting in more narrowly based candidates than might otherwise have been the case and working against coalition, is a major reason why in the five national elections since 1968, the Republicans have won four times, twice by authentic landslides, taking a grand total of 2,075 electoral votes against 567 for the Democrats, and carrying *every time* 22 states with a total of 202 electoral votes, only 68 short of victory. In the same five elections, the Democrats have carried *every time* the District of Columbia, with three electoral votes, 267 short of victory.

What's all this got to do with media?

Well, for one thing the so-called opening of the party dovetailed neatly with politicians' realization that television was becoming the dominant instrument of politics in large constituencies, certainly in national elections—a proposition demonstrated rather conclusively by the Nixon campaign in 1968. The power of television, and with it the power of the press generally, has blossomed in the new politics that followed 1968 and 1972.

Television was just right for primary candidates who needed to appeal not to a few party leaders but to the public, particularly those who were unknown outside their own states. But television appeals tend to emphasize personal qualities—looks, manner, one's degree of cool—other than experience, expertise, and proven leadership.

Television campaigning also was well suited to an era in which candidates had to seek many small contributions from the general public rather than a few large gifts from so-called fat cats. And as primaries proliferated, television advertising enabled candidates to campaign in several states at once—leading to such phenomena as a candidate sending a new batch of ads, rather than going personally, to shore himself up in some tight race. This week's Super Tuesday hardly would have been possible without television.

Televised debates, not just a high-noon shootout between the two general election finalists, but among candidates *en banc* and *ad infinitum* in the primary states, also are a dubious feature of this new era. Television has even spawned a new class—those professional managers, image makers, and "spin doctors" whose principal function is the manipulation of television viewers on behalf of political candidates, and one of whose major products is the upward spiraling cost of campaigning—owing to so much reliance on paid television.

On the other hand, television is not conducive or hospitable to coalition-building, deal-making, backroom arrangements, and the like. Television demands an open system, and an open system feeds on television. Don't be surprised if a deadlocked Democratic convention in Atlanta, should there be one this year, turns to negotiations not in a smoke-filled room but be-

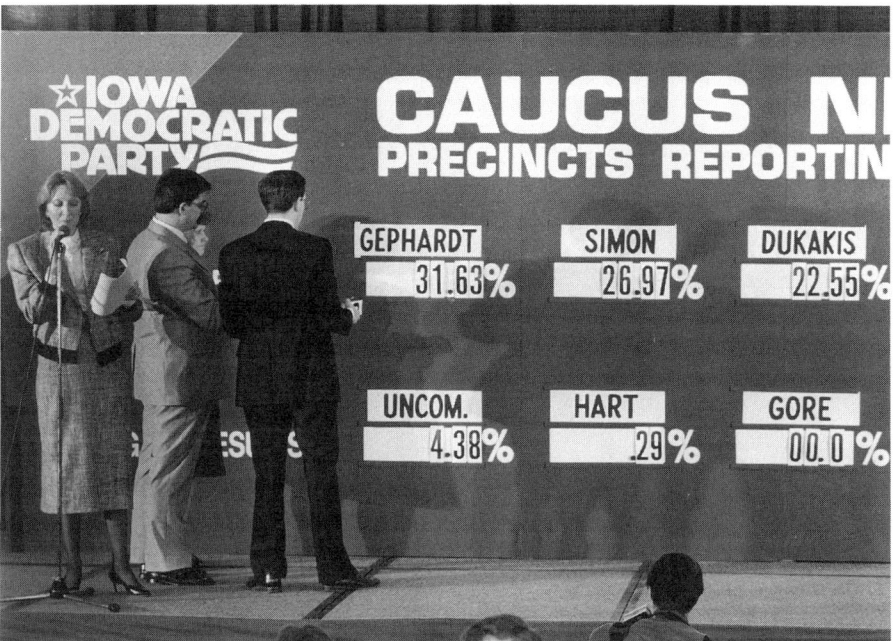

Early results in the 1988 Iowa presidential caucus.

fore a prime-time audience of millions, maybe with Tom Brokaw as moderator and calling time out for commercials.

But dwarfing all these developments, most of which were inevitable, is the circular influence of the media and the early primaries on each other, and on presidential politics.

If you have more than one primary or one set of state caucuses, there has to be a first. As every American over five years old must know, Iowa and New Hampshire offer the first tests in our system of choosing presidents—for no good reason that anyone can explain, other than that it might as well be them as, say, Oregon and Vermont, which would be equally unrepresentative.

A first test draws media as sugar draws flies. After months, perhaps years, of oratory, deadly-dull debates, contradictory polls, and conflicting claims between a dozen or more candidates—as in 1988—any kind of conclusive result is welcome. Not just television but newspapers and news magazines want results—numbers, winners, losers, candidates tearful or triumphant. Above all, we thirst for *drama*. Those first tests bring it to us the way a rescuer brings water to a man staggering in the desert.

The consequences of the disproportionate attention the media therefore pay to Iowa and New Hampshire are many and must to be questioned. Huge publicity and the image of a winner descends on a frontrunner—like Jimmy Carter, with his 28 percent of the Iowa vote in 1976—or even on someone who does better than predicted (predicted by the media, of course) as Gary Hart did when he won 16 percent of the Iowa vote in 1984.

That publicity and winner's image is worth a candidate's weight in contributions; people will give more eagerly to a perceived winner than to an also-ran. So the publicity, the image, and the contributions send the early winners off to a booming start in later contests.

On the other hand, the same media spotlight creates losers, too, and a losers' image makes as great a later impact as a winning image. What difference, in national terms, does it make that Richard Gephardt got about 4,000 more Democratic activists to attend caucuses in Iowa, a state with eight electoral votes, than Paul Simon did? That tells us little about the national electability of either man; but those few votes, as trumpeted to the world by the media, probably ruined Simon's national chances. They certainly were instrumental in his subsequent poor showings in New Hampshire and other early states.

Thus, media attention not only promotes the early tests far beyond their intrinsic importance, but that attention, not the tests themselves, makes or breaks candidacies. It produces "momentum"—immortalized as "Big Mo" by George Bush, when he thought he had it in 1980. And momentum can make these basically narrow early tests more important than primaries in major states—New York, Pennsylvania, Ohio, California—with bigger and more representative populations.

A study by Michael Robinson found that in 1976, "in proportionate terms," each Democratic vote in New Hampshire received 170 times as much network newstime as each Democratic vote later that year in New York. This year, the difference in network coverage of the Iowa caucuses from their later coverage of Super Tuesday, with 20 states voting and about a third of all delegates at stake, was not apparent to me. I haven't counted the column inches involved, but I expect the same was true of the *New York Times.* It's not that we shorted Super Tuesday; we just overplayedıIowa.

I don't contend that Iowa and New Hampshire, in combination with television and print, elect presidents. In fact, Jimmy Carter is the only winner of the Iowa caucuses ever to be elected president (save Nixon and Ronald Reagan as incumbents). This year, the Iowa Democratic winner, Gephardt, was the big loser on Super Tuesday; Bush, whose finish behind Bob Dole and Pat Robertson in Iowa nearly ruined his candidacy, was the big Republican winner, and Albert Gore, who scarcely campaigned in Iowa or New Hampshire, ran quite well in Super Tuesday states.

I do argue that Iowa and New Hampshire, in combination with outsize media coverage, produce results that warp the system and ought to cause those of us who have such a large hand in it to question that coverage. I've already mentioned Paul Simon's fate this year. Pat Robertson, on the other hand, was elevated in Iowa to clearly undeserved status as a "serious candidate." Michael Dukakis of Massachusetts, though his finances and organization probably made him a potential nominee in any case, got an enormous publicity boost for carrying New Hampshire, a huge number of whose citizens actually work in Massachusetts and watch that state's television.

Gore of Tennessee was written off as virtually a hopeless case when he decided to pass up Iowa and New Hampshire and concentrate on Super Tuesday. As it turned out, his strategy worked reasonably well and he's now touted as one of the three Democratic finalists, with Dukakis and Jesse Jackson.

What should concern those of us in the media is the extent to which we *create,* not merely report, the atmosphere in which

Choosing a President: Are Media Part of the Problem?

Al Gore, Jr., announcing that he would enter the race for the Democratic nomination for president in 1988.

such things happen. Because we put such emphasis on Iowa and New Hampshire, we propagated the notion that candidates had to do well in those tests. So when Gore, who had skipped them, won several states and a lot of delegates in the South, we reported that he had done "better than expected." That, as much as his third-place delegate total, makes him a winner again.

What are we now hearing and reading? That Gephardt is finished. Only a week ago a lot of those saying and writing that were saying and writing that Gephardt was one of the front-runners, sending the only "message" that the voters seemed to hear. So because he did *not* do as well as expected on Super Tuesday, we conclude that he's finished. He may be, but I fear that when Gephardt was the leader, as well as now that he's down, and when Gore was down as well as now that he's up, we in the media had more to do with it than we ought to have had.

I believe that broadcasting and print ought not to play so large a role in the selection of presidential candidates, and I don't think we have to. We could, for the best example, discipline ourselves not to cover the Iowa caucuses as if they were the Creation, and the New Hampshire primary as if it were the Second Coming.

All the arguments that the public demands such coverage, that the first tests are big tests, that the other networks and the newspapers are doing it, that we really have no choice—all those arguments really come down to one: that we see a big political story coming at last, and we move in for the kill.

I don't like to pass up a good story any more than any reporter does, but in Iowa and perhaps to a lesser extent New Hampshire, aren't we really making the story ourselves and not the voters? Isn't it our coverage that makes these tests "significant," and not their intrinsic national worth? And don't we claim in other cases—the treatment we give to presidential speeches, for example—the right of a free press to judge for itself what kind of coverage an event is worth?

We could and should make that kind of judgment about Iowa and New Hampshire, or whatever states might some year take their places. If we did, we'd not only be reducing our outsized influence on who ultimately wins and loses, we'd also be doing a more proper news job. I don't suggest any kind of collusion or concerted decision—just that each responsible news executive take it upon him or herself to make a responsible judgment. That's their job.

We could and should make greater efforts not to lend ourselves to the "expectations game." Here, it seems to me, is an area in which the public is sometimes justified in thinking the media overly interpretive; here we should listen, I believe, to the familiar lament: "Just give us the news, please."

Choosing a President: Are Media Part of the Problem?

It's true that that "new class" I spoke of works round the clock to put the right "spin" on primary results. These "sources" are often useful and informed, but they usually have an ax to grind, too. It may be that campaign coverage has to be horse-race coverage; but we don't have to give as much air and space to the touts, the tipsters, and the trainers as we do to the horses.

Political coverage always has been the richer for proper and informed speculation, but I question whether that should include setting the framework of expectations that, more with each passing election, seems to govern the fate of candidates. I find it truly disquieting that so often the expectation which the media say a candidate meets or fails to meet is an expectation largely created by that same media, playing both rules-maker and judge.

So if my fictional political boss returned from the past to look at the political writers and broadcasters of today, I'm not so sure he'd still say that we "provide a pretty good test." I'm afraid he might think, instead, that we're not so much the testers anymore as the arbiters. That's not a role news reporters should choose to play, nor allow themselves to fall into.

It's a fact of life, of course, that the news—what Woodrow Wilson called "the atmosphere of events"—will always play an important role in American politics. The power and reach of television, which has become something like the national nervous system, has made that role even more significant—I'd say dominant. But we in the press are not prisoners of some inexorable process; we still have the duty to consider what we're doing and the right to make necessary choices for ourselves.

The question I raise tonight is whether we're meeting that duty. If we're not, doesn't our claim to that right sound rather hollow?

8

Freedom and Responsibility: The Burden of the First Amendment

September 27, 1989

Perspective

The issue of press freedom is one that has emerged repeatedly over the course of this lecture series. John Chancellor decried the dangers of press restrictions during wartime, Henry Grunwald warned against the threat of libel suits, and most of the other lectures have tackled the issue in some way. Broadcast journalist Tom Brokaw, in the Eighth Chet Huntley Memorial Lecture, sheds a different light on the question of press freedom. Indeed, Brokaw suggests that perhaps the press has too much freedom—and too much power—for its own good.

There is no doubt that the mergers and acquisitions of press agencies have created a few mammoth organizations that dictate substantial amounts of the news material the public reads, hears, and watches. Brokaw is as attentive to these high-level corporate dealings as any informed "news junkie" would be. What he takes issue with is the way in which a powerful press, armed with its First Amendment freedoms, can all too easily turn into an irresponsible press. Freedom of the press—although it certainly serves a vital function in our society—can easily become a license for tabloid journalism. In other words, does one use constitutional law to support an expose regarding the Iran-Contra affair, or one regarding Bill Clinton and his alleged affair with Gennifer Flowers?

Tom Wicker, who spoke in the Huntley series the previous year, joins Brokaw in condemning irresponsible journalism. In 1988 he said, "I deplore the kind of thing that brought down Gary Hart and is threatening to bring down Bill Clinton. I don't think that sort of thing is relevant." The hardest issue in journalism today is the issue of encouraging reporters to be skeptical and investigatory, but then telling them that they have to stop at a certain point. It is almost an impossible thing to do. And tabloid journalism isn't merely the type that appears in recognized tabloids. It can creep into "respectable" newspapers and onto "quality" news shows, if editors are not careful to draw the line firmly.

The recent Clinton-Flowers case is an example of how the nontabloid media can seize upon a "hot item" that would generally remain in the hands of the more sensationalist news media. The article regarding the alleged love affair, based on "secret love [audio] tapes," initially appeared in the *Star*, a tabloid with a reputation for little more than celebrity gossip. Soon, however, without any evidence of the credibility of the tapes, the story developed into a media circus, with virtually every major news source running potentially damaging pieces about a candidate for the presidency.

At least, Brokaw pleads in his lecture, make sure the facts are straight before forging ahead. All too often, however, the invasion of private lives by the media does have a lasting effect on people's futures. It is impossible to know if Gary Hart would have succeeded in his presidential bid if he had been spared the stories of his marital infidelity, or if Michael Dukakis would have gained the White House if his wife Kitty had not been treat for alcoholism, but there is little doubt that such stories often contribute to the implosion of political careers. Tom Brokaw suggests that a close, public scrutiny of individual journalists could serve as a sobering reminder to them that the freedoms possessed by the press should be exercised responsibly. The First Amendment provides a safeguard for journalists so that they will have the freedom to pursue the task of effectively informing the public. With this freedom comes a duty to the public to act with due restraint and with the good of the people as their prime goal.

Introduction of Tom Brokaw by Edward Kosner

A native of Manhattan, Kosner began his journalism career at the New York Post *before moving on to a 16-year career as a writer and editor for* Newsweek. *He was named editor of* New York *in 1980 and went on to become the magazine's publisher (1986) and president (1991). Under his leadership,* New York *won four National Magazine awards and set records for circulation and advertising. Kosner was named editor-in-chief of* Esquire *in 1993.*

Introduction

Good evening ladies and gentlemen. It is a pleasure to introduce to you tonight a man of great talent and great charm—a man at the top of his profession. Tom Brokaw is that graceful, poised, competent human being we'd all like to be. It's appropriate that he's making the Eighth Chet Huntley Memorial Lecture tonight because it was the "Huntley-Brinkley Report" that first got him interested in journalism back in Webster, South Dakota, in the fifties.

He's been doing TV news since he was about twelve years old, in a dazzling career that's taken him from Omaha to Atlanta to Los Angeles, to the Watergate White House for NBC News, to the "Today Show," and, for the past seven years, he's been the anchorman of the "NBC Nightly News."

Two years ago he won the Triple Crown. He conducted the first TV interview with Mikhail Gorbachev on a Monday night; he refereed a presidential debate on a Tuesday night; and on Thursday night he joined the other anchors for an Oval Office interview with Ronald Reagan. In the midst of all this, John Chancellor took Brokaw aside and said, "You know about Friday, don't you?"

Brokaw didn't know. "The Vatican just called," said Chancellor. "He'll be in Jerusalem on Friday. You've got to be there!"

"Who?" Chancellor swears Brokaw wondered.

"Jesus Christ, of course," said Chancellor, "He's the only one that's left!"

The people who know Tom Brokaw best say that he remains a simple, small town kind of guy. Jeff Greenfield, ABC, says "Tom's really close to his roots. He keeps telling me how he tells that to the Pope and to Robert Redford all the time."

If there's anyone who is the rightful heir to the legacy of Chet Huntley, it's Tom Brokaw.

Tom Brokaw

Born February 6, 1940, in Webster, South Dakota, Tom Brokaw began his career in broadcast journalism with KMTV, NBC's Omaha, Nebraska, affiliate, in 1962. In 1965 Brokaw joined Atlanta's WSB-TV as editor and anchor of their nightly news broadcast, where he covered the burgeoning civil rights movement, occasionally contributing stories to the "Huntley-Brinkley Report." He moved to KNBC-TV in Los Angeles the following year, and five years later was named anchor of "First Tuesday," a monthly prime-time news show on NBC. He became NBC's White House correspondent in 1973, and anchor of the "Today Show" in 1976. Brokaw became sole anchor of "NBC Nightly News" in 1983, and has headed NBC's coverage of the three presidential campaigns since then. The first reporter to interview former Soviet premier Mikhail Gorbachev (December 1987), for which he won the Alfred I. DuPont Award, Brokaw has also hosted a number of other prime-time specials on such topics as securities trading, education, and homelessness.

Freedom and Responsibility: The Burden of the First Amendment

*P*ardon me if I feel unduly proud to be here tonight, the guest of honor at the Chet Huntley Lecture. After all, although he could not have been aware of it, Chet Huntley was a seminal force in my professional life. When the "Huntley-Brinkley Report" was first broadcast on NBC it was an epiphanous experience. I don't remember a single biinding moment of insight but I do recall a surge of excitement, thinking, "now there's something I'd like to be a part of." I was 15 at the time and I already knew the Dodgers were unlikely to hold second base open when my hero Jackie Robinson retired, so I was casting about for other suitable prospects.

Since my mind and mouth were always quicker than my feet and hands, journalism seemed a likely alternative. Later, in college, my friends recall me saying I'd like to have Chet Huntley's job someday. Middle-age modesty has blocked memory of such a specific dream, but I suppose it may be true. At that age ambition and ego are untempered by reality.

Certainly Chet and David were role models well before that phrase had currency. They delivered the news from distant places to my corner of rural America each night with grace and wit and insight.

Later I came to know David well personally, and although I met Chet only once or twice, he did not dispel my earlier impressions. He was serious about journalism but not too serious about himself, an unusual combination, especially given his celebrity status. Others who knew him better say he retained throughout the long, heady days of public adulation an uncommon touch for the common man, those Americans beyond the centers of power, without access to opinion columns and insider social gatherings, those Americans who rely on American journalism but remain a little leery of its style and practices. It is in the spirit of that memory of Chet Huntley that I appear before you tonight.

Let me begin with a fundamental truth known to all in my profession, an indisputable fact we seldom raise publicly. We're more inclined to discuss the perils of journalism than we are to acknowledge this fundamental truth: life as an American journalist is a life of privilege—an unlicensed profession with few statutory constraints and a powerful safeguard, the First Amendment. Moreover these are the conditions for journalists whatever their station. They come with the job, however modest or mighty the title.

There's another inherent privilege in journalism so obvious it is overlooked. We control the levers of criticism in this society. Criticism directed at our profession as well as criticism by our profession of other disciplines. Can anyone argue persuasively we treat both ends of that equation uniformly?

I think not. Ironically, I am persuaded that the unalloyed strengths of the First Amendment discourage critical analysis of the press by the press. Our freedom is so wide ranging we are not conditioned to external questions about our conduct. When they come we almost always act a little defensively, generally responding on the perimeters of our outlets. Earl Warren was fond of saying he read the sports page first because that's where mankind's achievements were recorded. The front page, he said, was reserved for mankind's failures.

The chief justice would have to look much harder to find where the newspaper's lapses were recorded. Equally true if he were looking for television's admissions of shortcomings. In American journalism we are inclined to call attention to everyone's failings but our own. When criticism is directed at us we develop what the late John Osborne liked to call journalism's glass jaw. We swing away but as soon as someone returns the punch, we drop to the floor, crying foul.

Oh, we construct occasional defenses against that charge. Letters to the editors. The occasional op-ed page piece. The

Freedom and Responsibility: The Burden of the First Amendment

Secretary of Defense Designate John Tower testifying before the Senate Armed Services Committee during his confirmation hearings in 1989. The Senate denied his confirmation.

American Society of Newspaper Editors recently chose to explore the subject of hype, sleaze, and professional credentials in a panel moderated by Fred Friendly. The panelists included Don Hewitt of "60 Minutes," Phil Donohue, Geraldo Rivera, Morton Downey, and others. It was wonderfully entertaining as it slipped into the same raucous behavior it was supposed to be examining, so raucous Mr. Downey had to plead for quiet.

To his credit, on other occasions, Fred Friendly assembles well-known journalists, First Amendment lawyers, and public and corporate figures to explore on public television the sticky ethical questions that are likely to come before them. The group dynamics are fascinating but I'm always a little disappointed the case studies are hypothetical. Isn't this just another form of simulation—about which we've been hearing a good deal recently.

Why not authentic cases—the USS Iowa investigation, the Barney Frank case, the John Tower hearings?

The John Tower case is representative of what concerns me. He is not a lovable man. He has behaved boorishly and drunkenly in public. He did have what could fairly be interpreted as a potential conflict of interest with defense contractors. Those are facts.

Nonetheless, a good deal more about John Tower was printed and broadcast. John Tower became a handy straw man for many journalists. A public figure gets in trouble or seems to be in trouble. An accusation, an unsubstantiated anecdote comes to the attention of a reporter. A few telephone calls fail to verify the details, but nonetheless it goes onto the air or into print with the caveat that it could not be corroborated. That reckless behavior is compounded when the uncorroborated fragment is then absorbed into America's broad, energetic information spectrum. It is whipped from one outlet to another, picking up weight and shape as it travels with lightning speed until it lands in someone's consciousness as a fact. Or in a computer file to be revived as a fact a later date.

That straw man approach is not the only egregious example of what happens when there is an undue reliance on unnamed sources. What should also be examined by the press in a public forum is the characterization of sources. Anonymity is so freely given, shouldn't we craft our characterizations with more care? "A middle level White House aide who's place in the hierarchy has been slipping today questioned the political agenda of more senior advisers."

In a recent issue of *Harpers*, Phil Weiss explored the Samuel Loring Morison case. Morison was arrested and convicted for sending classified pictures of Soviet ships to *Jane's Defense Weekly*. It turns out he was attempting in his own way to address personal concerns about what he perceived as the absence of U.S. urgency in dealing with Soviet naval expansion. As Weiss reconstructs the initial coverage of the case, however, he reprints a portion of a newspaper story at the time of Morison's arrest. The paper quoted a government source as saying, "This isn't a leak case, this is a guy who's in it for the dough." As Weiss concludes, the source was inaccurate, calculated, and persuasive. He's not the only government source who's been all three. It happens every day.

And it happens not just in the government, but in private sector as well. Although it is difficult to quantify, I am persuaded there's an expanding tendency of reporters to offer cover quickly, whatever the circumstances. And the cover is often airtight. "Insider" is a favorite. It may mean only the source works inside the same building.

That is not to say unnamed sources are unacceptable or unimportant. Indeed, they are crucial to the free flow of information, but they should be subjected to the same tests as the primary subjects of a story. What is the motivation of the unnamed sources? Were they in the room when the decision was made? Are they passing along second-hand, uncorroborated information which then is then diluted one more time before it gets on the air or into print? The offer of anonymity ought to come last not first, and when it is offered it should not be a permissive gesture.

I have my own secondary descriptions for the various phases of attribution. When a source is willing to go on the record it is not necessarily a sign of courage; it generally means he or she expects some acclamation. When they say "I want to talk to you on background," it often means a score is about to be evened. Under the rules, deep background precludes the reporter from offering even a general description of the primary source. This is the darkened field from which trial balloons are launched. And when you hear, "I want to go off the record," be especially wary. It often means the subject knows you have the goods—and in desperation he or she will confirm but only off the record, in a fashion you're honor bound not to use it.

The unnamed source. At least as worthy of press examination, print and electronic, as those annual stories about congressional junkets or honoraria. For the unnamed source and how it is used is an important strut in the framework of our integrity.

It is not only our conduct that must be subjected to greater self-examination. That same disinfectant, sunshine, Louis Brandeis immortalized, should more regularly be directed at the institutions of the press. *Time* magazine is now a piece of the largest communications entertainment conglomerate in history and when the courtship was about to be consummated, *Time* was indefensibly mute. Rupert Murdoch, owner of the Fox Television Network, buys *TV Guide* and there is almost no discussion of the potential conflict.

Broadcast institutions and broadcast journalism undergo a more rigorous examination, in part because of the public air waves factor, in part because they occupy such a prominent place in the popular culture, and in part because the structure of broadcast journalism offends the sensibilities of many print traditionalists. Fairly, television news invites the nature of much of the criticism it receives by promotion that is at once self-congratulatory and personality intensive.

As a result, criticism of broadcast television in print is a kind of blood sport in which the object too often seems to be to kill or maim rather than examine. Lest you think I speak only as a wounded quarry, let me emphasize that I think it is healthy and useful to have a regular exposition of the electronic news media. If only newspapers and magazines were as eager to examine each other. Whenever I suggest that to my newspaper friends they become uncharacteristically self-deprecating and try to persuade me the public would not be interested. They are unjustly modest. These are the same papers that regularly examine the merits of books by little known authors, books that will be read by only a fraction of the number of people who will see the newspaper every day. The same editors who regularly transform anonymous figures with pale personalities caught in some unexpected chain of events into larger than life villains or heroes in a three-column spread on page one, section two. Dead playwrights and dying athletes come alive on their pages but, no, the public wouldn't be interested in the lives of or the interests of or the decision-making process of the people who perform this daily alchemy.

Nonsense. Especially since the consolidation of newspaper ownership in this country they represent ever greater concentrations of press power.

If they choose not to subject themselves to outside examination, if they decide not to cooperate, indeed, if they try to discourage the process, so be it. The First Amendment also entitles a subject to say "no." Other newspapers or broadcast journalists who judge them newsworthy should not give up the hunt, however.

There are some encouraging signs. Eleanor Randolph of the *Washington Post,* Alex Jones of the *New York Times,* David Shaw of the *Los Angeles Times* are gifted and enterprising reporters. Their bylines are appearing more regularly over stories about specific controversies within other newspapers and the news decision-making process.

The decision of Bill Kovach to leave the *Atlanta Constitution,* the intramural debate within the *New York Daily News* over a mayoral endorsement, the place of *USA Today* in the national newspaper spectrum—all stories that made it into the sunshine, and the integrity of the press was not compromised. I could argue that it was strengthened. During the recent debate over the place of simulation—or reconstruction or reenactment or faking it, whatever phrase you like—on television news programs, almost nothing was heard from broadcast journalists about a topic that reflected, in one way or another, on all of them. Heard on their own programs, that is. Certainly the topic was getting a great deal of attention in the corridors and around the water cooler. It was a topic worthy of examination on the air as well as behind the scenes in television news. Other questions about press conduct also are worthy—the portrayal of minorities in the mostly white American news media, the invasion of the private lives of innocent victims of tragedy, the intimate details of the private lives of public figures, not just politicians. What about sports stars and other icons of the popular culture? The list is long and provocative.

Do not be misled by these observations. I am not an advocate of the timid, apologetic approach of news. I believe in Wilbur Story, the celebrated Chicago editor who said a newspaper's duty is to print the news and raise hell. I also believe we who are involved in that particular form of hellraising are not immune from criticism and examination. I would like to think the process and the product deserve more attention than the personalities, but I am realistic enough to understand that is unlikely. So a simple plea for a little more of the former and a little less of the latter.

The American news media are so powerful and now so pervasive in the every day lives of viewers and readers we cannot pretend we are incidental to their interests. Gratefully, they seem to approve of most of what we do. In a recent Gallup poll for the *Los Angeles Times,* almost 80 percent of those questioned said they believed journalists care about the quality of their work, 72 percent judged us to be highly professional, and 54 said we are moral. However, 55 percent said we try to cover up our mistakes. Cover them up. And 53 percent believe we're often influenced by the powerful. Seventy-five percent believe public figures are entitled to the same protection from libel as private citizens. And just over half—55 percent—believe we get the facts straight. Five-fifty will win the major league batting title, but in the hardball we play, is that an average that makes us proud?

Oh, sure, I know we're only as good as our sources. One man's fact is another man's lie. Bias, like beauty, is in the eye of the beholder. I've used them all.

But I also know a lot of journalists who themselves have been the subjects of newspaper or television news stories. It's too often a shocking or painful experience. The little, easily determined facts that go wildly astray—like dates and names and quotes. If the easy part gets fouled up, what about the larger conclusion or interpretations.

Freedom and Responsibility: The Burden of the First Amendment

Dr. Harold Agnew, who ran the Los Alamos Weapons Laboratory, had what I always believed was a sensible scheme for making political leaders aware of the dangers of nuclear weapons. He said every time a new leader rises to power anywhere in the world they should be brought to the South Pacific, placed on an atoll, stripped of their clothing and made to stand with their back turned to a low-yield nuclear detonation some miles off. Even at that distance—and even with a small explosion, he said—they would feel the enormous force and heat of nuclear power. Then they would have a practical, personal appreciation of it's destructive capability.

Were it left to me I would adapt a similar ceremony for journalists. Instead of exposing them to nuclear power, I would arrange for every newcomer to this grand calling to be the subject of a newspaper or television news story about their personal background, qualifications, and motivation. It is a ritual which should be repeated every ten years or so during their careers. So they could have a personal appreciation of the effect of their work.

The First Amendment is a sacred law, a secular canon in the liturgy of individual rights, a political, religious, and press freedom. It protects us from unjust laws, but it cannot protect us from ourselves. Only we can do that.

9

Crime, the Masses, and Media Responsibility

November 8, 1990

Perspective

Rare are the critics that question media magnate Rupert Murdoch's business savvy. His accomplishments are impressive, spanning from the United States to Australia, with few areas in between left untouched. Many have argued, however, that his products—from newspapers like the *New York Post* to television shows such as Fox's "A Current Affair"—have lowered the quality of journalism, or at least lowered the expectation of quality journalism, on a massive scale. In his appearance at the Chet Huntley Memorial Lecture Series, Murdoch counters his most vehement detractors in the media establishment.

Crime, the Masses, and Media Responsibility

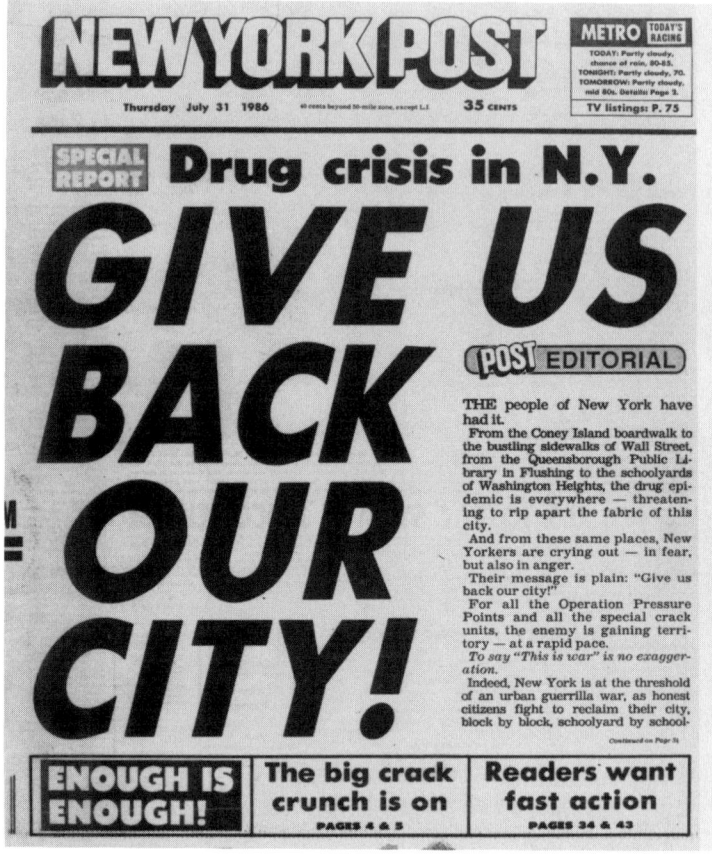

In his lecture, Murdoch quotes from Osborn Elliot, dean of Columbia's Journalism School, who once wrote that the *New York Post* appealed "to the basest passions and appetites of the hour." As Murdoch points out, however, such criticism is as much an attack on the "downmarket" audience, tending demographically to be based largely on the working classes, as it is on his *New York Post*. The simple fact that wide audiences choose to read newspapers like the *Boston Herald* (one of only several newspapers that Murdoch still owns in the United States) and watch television programs like "A Current Affair" should give some indication that the issues presented in these forums are considered significant to millions of Americans.

Perspective

The same is true of popular "downmarket" media sources in other countries. Intellectual elitism, Murdoch suggests, is as pervasive as liberalism in the news media. Not only does this exclusionary attitude indicate an exclusionary principle at work in the "respectable" news media, it suggests a lack of interest, or perhaps a fear, of publicizing the issues that popular audiences find important.

One of these issues that the liberal news media often downplay is crime, particularly as it occurs in the heart of America's media capital, New York City. Murdoch suggests that his critics should spend less time thumbing their noses at the "ordinary readers" who show a justifiable concern about the crime in their streets, and more time thinking and writing about the crime itself. Murdoch points to a police force that has been shrinking since the mid-1970s and to a 25 percent jump in crime in New York City between 1975 and 1990. New York has consistently come close to, or topped, a rate of 2,000 murders per year in recent times, and robberies average 100,000 per year. With statistics like this—and, admittedly, New York has not been alone in its experience of the rising tide of crime—Murdoch asks, "Where are the journalists?" Why, he asks, are they avoiding an issue that affects virtually everyone? He argues that in today's world, we all need to know about crime so that we can protect ourselves, our families, and our neighborhoods from victimization. Media that serve this function should not be looked down upon.

Crime, the Masses, and Media Responsibility

Introduction of Rupert Murdoch by Michael Gartner

Former NBC News president Michael Gartner has a long history in journalism. An editor for many years with the Wall Street Journal, *and more recently a columnist with* USA Today, *Gartner has also worked with major newspapers in Des Moines, Louisville, and Ames, Iowa. A former chairman of the Pulitzer Prize board, he served as president of NBC News from 1988 to 1993. He introduces Rupert Murdoch for the Ninth Chet Huntley Memorial Lecture.*

Introduction

I am here to introduce Rupert Murdoch, who is a charming billionaire—and you'd think that would be enough for anyone. Certainly, I'd settle for either charming or billionaire, though I do have a preference.

But that is not enough for Rupert Murdoch. Add to the charm and the billions a courage and a vision: a courage to take risks that is rarely found in businessmen and a vision of the future that is found even less often. He operates a media empire that has legs in Australia, where he was born and where he owns more than one hundred newspapers and—oddly—an airline; and England, where he owns five national newspapers and eight magazines and a satellite TV service; and America, where he lives as a naturalized citizen. He controls companies that own *New York* Magazine and *TV Guide* and the *Boston Herald* and HarperCollins and 20th-Century Fox and Fox Television and *The Daily Racing Form* and *Seventeen* magazine, among other things. He is responsible for Bart Simpson and the *Times* of London. Make what you will of that!

At age 59, he is the very model of a modern major media mogul. Indeed, he and his businesses represent the very complexity of the media world today. Time was when one person owned this and another owned that. The relationships were clear—one person competed with another, sometimes genteelly, sometimes fiercely.

One other thing—Mr. Murdoch's companies are said to have some cash flow problems and their debt is said to be more than eight billion dollars. We are indebted to you tonight for coming here, Mr. Murdoch, but in all honesty, I must tell you that the honorarium isn't going to get you out of any jams.

Rupert Murdoch

Born March 11, 1931, in Melbourne, Australia, Rupert Murdoch is the son of a newspaper publisher. He began his media empire in the early 1950s with one newspaper in the small, southern Australian city of Adelaide. The Adelaide News *became a huge success, and Murdoch went on to purchase a number of other Australian newspapers. In 1964 he founded a national newspaper, the* Australian. *His media empire grew, reaching towards England by the late 1960s and to the shores of America in the 1970s. A listing of Murdoch's countless sales and acquisitions of newspapers, magazines, book publishing houses, and film and television production industries could fill an entire book. In the United States he is perhaps best known for his acquisition of 20th-Century Fox and the subsequent merger of that company with Metromedia to create the highly successful Fox television network, "the fourth network," which has rating patterns that match CBS, NBC, and ABC. A number of biographers have attempted to chart the series of events that has made Murdoch a global media magnate. The most recent biography,* Murdoch (1993), *by British journalist William Shawcross, is considered to be among the best. Most recently, Murdoch reacquired the* New York Post, *which he had sold in 1988.*

Crime, the Masses, and Media Responsibility

*I*t is indeed a pleasure and an honor for me to be invited to deliver the annual Chet Huntley Memorial Lecture here at New York University, the home, as I understand it, of the second oldest journalism department in the country.

I'm particularly pleased to deliver this lecture for a couple of reasons that may be peculiar to myself.

Firstly, the memory of Chet Huntley is inextricably associated with the development and the first true flowering of television and television news.

Now, like Mr. Gartner, I come from a print family. One of my earliest childhood memories is watching my father lying in bed in the morning, going through the paper he published, the *Melbourne Herald,* slashing at it with a pen and scribbling notes on it that would later become helpful missives to his various editors. I still do this myself. I've often said that my heart really belongs to newspapers.

But I suppose it would equally be true to say that my head belongs to television. I am morally convinced that, whatever we may think, we've only just begun to see the revolution that this medium, which is after all still very young, will effect on society and on the way we live. And I've acted on this conviction, of course, with Fox Broadcasting, the nascent fourth network, here in the U.S., and with Sky television, our five satellite channels, in the U.K.

Whatever the ultimate ramifications of television, however, whatever direction it takes, the influence of Chet Huntley and David Brinkley will always be discernable, just as the tree leans where the twig is bent.

Rupert Murdoch

So this is one reason that I feel a personal interest in commemorating Chet Huntley's achievement here today.

My second personal reason for feeling honored by this invitation is that the "Huntley-Brinkley Report" was, after all, a very American institution. Americans may take for granted the warm welcome that this country offers to immigrants. But I think I speak for most immigrants, ladies and gentlemen, when I assure you that we do not take it for granted, and we do not forget.

And this brings me to the topic I wanted to address tonight.

Last year, Tom Brokaw said here that, and I quote, "I am persuaded that the unalloyed strengths of the First Amendment discourage critical analysis of the press by the press in America. Our freedom is so wide ranging that we are not conditioned to external questions about our conduct." I agree with this sentiment, although I'm less sure about one of the examples Tom gave: my own acquisition of *TV Guide*. He suggested this posed a "potential conflict of interest." Now I must say that, as far as my own activities are concerned at least, I've never felt that there's been a lack of what Tom termed "critical analysis." Or, for that matter, criticism without analysis. Thus in the case of *TV Guide,* for example, there are as a practical matter fierce competitive constraints on what any management could do, even if it wanted to abuse its position, which we emphatically do not. Nevertheless, I think Tom was on to something. And I propose to continue tonight in the critical tradition he has established.

I want to talk about the current crime crisis in New York City, and the role of the media in its development.

When I listen to some recent commentary on New York, I am reminded of the kind of Old Testament text that my Scottish grandfather, who was a Presbyterian clergyman and a child of the Victorian Era, might have made the basis of a resounding sermon. See if you recognize New York in the Prophet Nahum's considered opinion of the Assyrian capital of Nineveh, which I'll give in the King James version:

> Woe to the bloody city! It is all full of lies and robbery; the prey departeth not; the noise of a whip, and the noise of the rattling

of the wheels, and of the prancing horses, and of the jumping chariots. . . . There is no healing of thy bruise; thy wound is grievous; all that hear the bruit of thee shall clap the hands over thee: for upon whom hath not thy wickedness passed continually?

Well, New York is the media capital, so our problems do tend to get bruited about the country. And who knows? It's even possible that the rest of America feels we've been continually passing wickedness upon them. But New Yorkers are a hardy lot. I think that, at any rate until recently, they would just have dismissed Nahum by reflecting: at least we don't have a chariot problem.

But we really do have a crime problem. We've all rationalized it for years, We've said that it's part of a worldwide pattern, or that its not the worst in American on a per capita basis, or even that people who go on about crime are hysterics, and worse. But the truth is, ladies and gentlemen, that the crime problem in New York is quite simply horrible. In fact, it seems to be unprecedented in American history.

It's certainly worse than the Wild West. The other day, I was shown a study of the California frontier, called *Gunfighters, Highwaymen & Vigilantes,* by Professor Roger McGrath. It demonstrated that while the murder rate on the frontier was high, it was almost entirely confined to certain groups of what Professor McGrath called "consenting adults," notably of young miners and cowboys. It almost never affected innocent people. And crimes like robbery and rape were far more infrequent than today.

And New York's crime problem is far worse than in other countries. Its homicide rate is 10 times higher than London's, 15 times higher than Toronto's, 30 times higher than Tokyo's. It's as if history has suddenly started to run backward. The long trend toward a more ordered and civilized society in America, which continued right through the worst of the depression and the war and into the 1950s, has decisively reversed.

If I can quote from an exhaustive survey by Jonathan Greenberg which we published in *New York* magazine in September:

> Major crime exploded during the sixties and seventies, peaking during the late seventies and early eighties . . . during the mid-eighties, crime dropped off [slightly]—a development [that can be attributed] to a decline in the number of youths in the city and an increase in the size of the police force. But the rates have now come roaring back. This year, for the third year in a row, New York will easily surpass all historical highs for homicide. Robbery and auto theft may also set new records.

One measure of the magnitude of New York's crime problem is that in this city there are annually almost 2,000 murders. That's a bit less than half the number of Americans killed on average in each year of the Vietnam War. Just in New York. Indeed, I don't think it's out of place to describe what's going on, in New York and in America today, as a silent Vietnam. After all, for young black men, homicide has become the leading cause of mortality.

Now this is a profound tragedy. It's something I'm sure you all feel personally, because New York is a city that tends to mean a great deal to those of us who have fallen under the spell it can cast—or could cast.

If I can give you my own perspective again, New York represented an enormous liberation to Anna and myself when we first came here in 1973. There were a lot of reasons for this. We had been living in London, and we found society there to be much more cold, confining, and in some sense unfriendly to outsiders. Of course, this may just be a reflection of my warm, expansive, and amiable personality. But in any case, New York suited us beautifully. In those days my office was down on Third Avenue, and at the end of the day we would take enormous pleasure in simply walking along arm-in-arm, taking in the street scene, browsing among the shops, choosing from among the endless variety of small restaurants—the kind of thing you've all done. Anna went back to school here, at New York University, ultimately getting her Master's Degree. And that's another thing that was easier than in England, not just because the educational institutions were more enlightened about making it possible for the mothers of small children to attend, but also because it struck nobody as odd or eccentric or deserving of sneering comment.

In fact, as I think about it now, it was not just the celebrated energy of New York that appealed to us, but the freedom resulting from its very atomism and anonymity—the exact qualities that have often been decried in modern cities. In some sense, New York was the ultimate modern city, just as American society generally is the ultimate expression of the process of modernization.

Well, we don't find the New York street scene much fun any more. And naturally I ask myself, "How did this happen?" or to put it more specifically, "Why hasn't this tragedy dominated politics and compelled the attention of our elected officials to the point where they stepped in and actually did something about it?"

Obviously, one part of the answer is that the crime problem has developed gradually. The overall change has been dramatic—Central Park was safe well within living memory, but the year-to-year deterioration was relatively small and human beings can be led a long way one step at a time.

But the media should not have been gradually led anywhere. We are supposed to be alert to social change. It's news, and it also determines the nature of our audience, which pays our way.

Crime has been reported, of course. But there hasn't been the sustained campaigning coverage that you get when journalists, editors, and publishers really decide that an issue is a major story. Instead, coverage has been intense only spasmodically and erratically.

Occasional particularly atrocious crimes—the Central Park rape, the Times Square subway stabbing—have unpredictably acquired enormous symbolic importance. This has greatly irritated the overly rational and the overly complacent, who point out that similarly awful crimes occur all the time and are more or less ignored.

Rupert Murdoch

The media has been hovering between its instinct for a vital story, on the one hand, and powerful inhibitions on the other. And I believe this is another part of the answer to the question of why the crime issue has never really crystallized in politics: the media's inhibitions about reporting the crime wave resulted in a sort of false consciousness among the public. Its outrage was not invited and directed. Its apprehensions remained individual and inchoate.

In other words, ladies and gentlemen, to a certain extent I blame myself for what's happened to New York. After all, I owned the *New York Post* from 1976 to 1988. And newspapers, above all other media, have traditionally been the preeminent forum for venting an issue of this kind: they have the frequency, the space, and the readership.

When I bought the *Post*, I found myself portrayed on the cover of *Time* magazine as King Kong. The *Time* editors supplied what they imagined was a typical tabloid headline. In huge type it read: "Extra!!! [with three exclamation points] Aussie Press Lord terrifies New York."

Maybe it was true. When we front-paged the looting that followed the 1977 New York blackout, Osborn Elliot, then a deputy mayor in the Beame administration, wrote an open letter in the *New York Times* accusing me of cheapening American journalism. Later, when he was dean of Columbia's Journalism School, the *Columbia Journalism Review* editorialized that the *Post* appealed "to the basest passions and appetites of the hour." The editorial concluded "the *New York Post* is no longer a journalistic problem. It is a social problem—a force for evil." The headline was "Doing the Devil's Work."

Rough stuff for the grandson of a Presbyterian minister.

In fact, of course, as the professionals in this audience will recognize, we never took the *New York Post* as far downmarket (to use the technical term, which seems to me in itself to imply disdain for ordinary readers) as the early American tabloids. Or even as far as *Sun* in London, where we face ferocious competition from other popular papers.

And I have a different definition of the devil's work. It's what happened in Central Park and in the Times Square subway

Crime, the Masses, and Media Responsibility

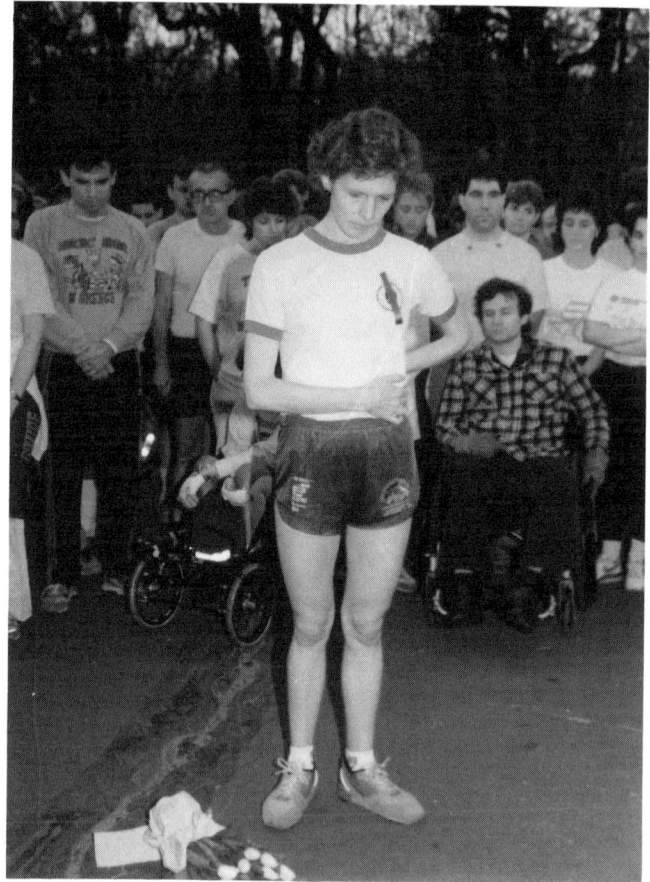

A moment of silence at the spot where a woman jogger was raped and beaten in New York's Central Park.

station, and what is happening on the streets of New York City every day, right now, in the few minutes we've been gathered here.

I don't accept that the public's outrage over these atrocities is a "base passion," or that its cry for justice is a "base appetite." When I consider what was developing in New York during my ownership of the *Post* and in the years since its sale, I don't agree that I took it too far downmarket. I think I didn't take it downmarket far enough.

What, generally, are these inhibitions that have affected newspapers coverage of crime?

One is institutional. When a newspaper has a monopoly, as in most American cities, or even when its competition is limited, as is now the case in New York, the logical strategy is blandness, to avoid controversy that might upset powerful interest groups. Only where there's real competition is there an incentive to choose between interests and to remain sensitive to the public's concerns no matter how unfashionable in the press club, the country club, and the caucus room.

One of the most powerful factors making for monopoly is what economists call "barriers to entry." In the newspaper business, this usually means the printing unions. They enforce salary levels and, even worse, unproductive practices that make it prohibitively expensive to start new papers. They do this even though in the long run new papers would mean more work for everybody.

As you will know, in 1986 I took on the printing unions in Britain, the world's worst, and broke them. The result has been a silver age for British journalism: newly prosperous papers and wholly new papers. I'm sure these papers feel very grateful to me, although some have not shown much sign of it.

With the demise of the British print unions, the New York City unions have succeeded to the distinction of being the world's worst. And, of course, the *Daily News* is on strike at the moment. I don't know what the outcome will be. But I will say this: we won in Britain because that country had courageous political leadership.

The government had passed laws that reduced the privileged position of the labor unions, particularly with regard to the secondary picketing and the violence and intimidation which they had come to depend upon. The police, at some real risk to themselves, were prepared to enforce those laws. The fate of New York's newspaper industry will in the end be determined by whether this city's political leadership has that kind of courage.

Crime, the Masses, and Media Responsibility

A second inhibition that affects the media's coverage of crime is a matter of professional mores. Journalists are not machines, however preferable that might sometimes appear. Their individual and collective predelictions quite often matter more than those of the poor publisher, who is after all distracted by the need to sell advertisements, placate print unions, and so on.

I had a reminder of this just recently. I thought our *Boston Herald* had endorsed John Silber, the combative president of Boston University, for the governorship of Massachusetts. But Dr. Silber felt, strongly, that we were opposing him, because of the coverage he was getting in our news columns. As it turns out, the people of Massachusetts appear to have agreed with our news rather than our editorials.

Well, what are the professional mores of journalism? It is a curious fact, amply demonstrated by sociologists like Professor Stanley Rothman of Smith College, that the elite media is overwhelmingly on the left side of the political spectrum. Rothman's survey found, for example, that in the presidential elections of 1964 through 1976, never less than 80 percent of journalists and editors in the elite media voted Democratic and never more than 19 percent Republican, even though the Republicans won two of the races, one in a landslide, and the third was almost a tie.

Now I don't want anyone to think that I'm complaining about this. After all, I bought *The Village Voice* by accident and sold it for $58 million. But it obviously has significant consequences for the media's judgment of news.

For example, many of you will have seen Walter Wriston's article in the *Wall Street Journal* last week. Walter pointed out, very effectively, that what he called the "beltway-media" complex has succeeded in establishing a number of conventional wisdoms about the economy as unimpeachable fact, when they are actually quite untrue. Thus it's untrue to say that social spending was cut in the Reagan years; it actually rose. And it's untrue to say that there was a decrease in the share of taxes paid by the rich; their share actually increased. Many of you will have the opposite impression. This is not because journalists are deliberately lying to you, particularly, it's just that their values lead them, often quite unconsciously, to accept certain assumptions rather than others.

And this inhibition that results from values has played its role in the media's attitude to the New York story. For example, when a young black man was shot and killed by white youths in Bensonhurst, the *Daily News* headlined its editorial "Dare to Attack Racist Violence." When the Central Park rape occurred, the *Daily News* headed its editorial: "Keep Calm, New York." This sense of news values may have been right, but it was unmistakably political.

Which brings us to the extreme taboo, pervading the entire political culture, about any discussion that is deemed to approach the subject of race. This is an acute difficulty in the case of crime because, as Jonathan Greenburg for example reported in his *New York* magazine article, blacks made up 24 percent of New York's population and 57 percent of those arrested for homicide last year; whites made up 45 percent of the population and just 8.8 percent of the homicide arrests. Greenburg also pointed out that the overwhelming majority of black homicides were against other blacks. But nevertheless *New York* still received, and published, bitter criticism that these facts were mentioned at all.

I think we have to admit the sad reality: the media shied away from reporting crime because it feared exacerbating racial tension. We did not believe that the truth would set us, and society at large, free.

There's a famous story about the *New York Post* which I'm wearily convinced you've all heard. The management of Bloomingdale's was supposed to have explained their refusal to advertise with us by saying, "Your readers are our shoplifters."

Over the years, I've become very tired of denying this ever happened. From long experience, I suspect it was invented by journalists over an expense account drink, perhaps paid for by me. But it was one of those myths that tapped a mood, and perhaps I can now get my money's worth by directing your attention to the implicit contempt, pervasive throughout the

New York media and political elites, that it revealed for the ordinary families who bought the *Post* in greatly increased numbers while we ran it, to say nothing, of course, of the considerable number of yuppies and Wall Streeters who read it for relaxation on the train home.

One final observation, about television and crime coverage, since this is the Chet Huntley Memorial Lecture and since I own Fox and WNYW here in New York.

I said earlier that newspapers have been the traditional forum for venting an issue of this kind. But actually there's no technical reason why television couldn't play this role even better. The reason television does not play this role is entirely political. Currently, public policy requires that each station's place in the broadcast spectrum be allocated though a licensing process, that is, in effect, by politicians.

In return for this privilege, the television industry accepts significant restrictions on its First Amendment rights—for example, the FCC's "Fairness Doctrine" which the Congress is trying to restore. These inhibitions essentially preclude editorial campaigns and generally leave the industry much more at the mercy of political interests than are newspapers.

The more I think about it, the more I think the whole rationale for setting up a licensing system was always fundamentally flawed. The theory was that the broadcast spectrum was limited and that therefore government had to step in to prevent chaotic competition and to safeguard the public interest.

But so is Manhattan real estate limited, and we allow that to be allocated by the free market, more or less. Indeed, if Washington established property rights in the spectrum and auctioned it off, the Treasury could receive significant financial benefit, particularly if the property was leasehold. Or maybe the federal budget is no longer a concern.

In any case, the advent of satellites and cable television is now making possible the reception of possible dozens, even hundreds, of channels. In other words, the argument for licensing and regulating the broadcasting media will increasingly be seen to be the same as the argument for licensing and regulating the press. And, as any graduate from NYU's journalism department can tell you, that was settled a long time ago.

Let me now summarize my argument.

The development of the crime problem in New York is a peculiar case where the market for truth did not seem to clear. Most people were distressed about crime, but their distress somehow did not translate into a political will to do something about it.

The reasons for this were what Senator Moynihan once called, in the days before he became a statesman, "a tangle of pathologies." But I believe a key part of the problem was the existence of institutional and professional inhibitions in the media, above all a disdain for the popular press and, ultimately, for ordinary people.

Accordingly, a key part of the solution is more freedom, and less disdain.

In the meantime, if anyone wants to buy a penthouse overlooking Central Park that's worth distinctly less than it was three years ago, please come up and see me afterwards.

PN 4888 .T4 V54 1994